100 Secrets for Living a Life You Love
Finding Happiness Despite Life's Roadblocks

by *Jonathan Lockwood Huie*

ife You Love

8/14

ISBN: 978-1-44959-511-1

Jonathan Lockwood Huie
www.DreamThisDay.com
www.JonathanLockwoodHuie.com
jlh@jlhuie.com

About the Author

Jonathan Lockwood Huie, consultant, speaker, personal coach, lover of life, and co-author of *Simply An Inspired Life*, is known as "The Philosopher of Happiness."

Mr. Huie writes the popular *Daily Inspiration - Daily Quote* which is available on-line at **www.DreamThisDay.com** and via free email subscription.

For 30 years, Mr. Huie was a highly successful technologist and executive of Silicon Valley start-up companies, bearing titles such as Senior Vice President and Chief Architect. After one of his start-ups was acquired in 2000, Jonathan directed his attention toward the human issues of happiness, life satisfaction, work-life balance, and cooperative behavior (teamwork).

Mr. Huie is pleased to receive your email at jlh@jlhuie.com

Jonathan Lockwood Huie
www.DreamThisDay.com
www.JonathanLockwoodHuie.com
jlh@jlhuie.com

Also by Jonathan Lockwood Huie

Simply An Inspired Life: Consciously Choosing Unbounded Happiness in Good Times and Bad - co-authored with Mary Anne Radmacher - Conari Press 2009.

Regaining Your Happiness in Seven Weeks e-Training Program
www.DreamThisDay.com/happiness-program

Daily Inspiration - Daily Quote
Sign-up at www.DreamThisDay.com to receive Jonathan's *Daily Inspiration - Daily Quote* free via email.

Table of Contents

100 Secrets for Living a Life You Love

The writings of Jonathan Lockwood Huie are based solely upon his life experiences and are his opinions. Consult an appropriate medical professional for any issues of physical or emotional health.

Introduction

Play with life, laugh with life, dance lightly with life, and smile at the riddles of life, knowing that life's only true lessons are writ small in the margin.
 - Jonathan Lockwood Huie

You *can* live the life you love - even in the face of the most challenging circumstances. While sometimes it may appear that life throws more obstacles in your path than you can handle, you can always choose to be happy. Yes, you are that powerful.

What if you lost your job, your house burned down, the creditors are closing in, and your marriage has become hellishly confrontational? Is it possible to maintain a positive outlook under such stress and strain? Yes, happiness is always a choice.

This book consists of 100 independent "secrets" that provide the keys to living the life you love. Many of these secrets were originally published in modified form as *Daily Inspirations* on the www.DreamThisDay.com website.

You can read the secrets in sequence, open the book randomly, or scan the table of contents for help with today's challenge. It is intentional that some "secrets" are inspiring and reassuring, while others challenge your core beliefs and stimulate your thinking.

Consider adopting the ongoing practice of reading and contemplating one "secret" each day.

There will be days when you say, "That's obvious, everybody knows that." Let those days be a gentle reminder.

There will be days when the "secret" makes you feel good, and you say, "Ah." Let those days be tranquil and comforting.

There will be days when you say, "Huh, what does that mean?" Let those be days of inquiry and questioning.

There may be days when you say, "NO WAY! That doesn't agree with my view of how things should be." Let those be days to contemplate, question, and then listen to your own heart and mind. Only you can choose your beliefs and behaviors.

Thank you for joining me in this journey we call life,
 Jonathan

Jonathan Lockwood Huie
www.DreamThisDay.com   www.JonathanLockwoodHuie.com   jlh@jlhuie.com

Positive Affirmations

by Jonathan Lockwood Huie

- I live with enthusiasm, and give thanks for my life.

- I release the familiar that I may better discover my inspiring future.

- I CHOOSE with Open Mind and Open Heart.

- I have ready access to a power beyond my wildest imagination.

- I forgive everyone, especially myself, for all actions and all inactions throughout my entire life.

- I radiate my kindness into the world.

- Standing in the inspiring vision of my future, I boldly take every step - large and small - with courage and intent.

- I put aside personal preferences and step forward to be of service.

- I see the miracle in all of life. I am thankful for all creation.

- I gratefully accept the light and pay it forward.

- I follow my own star and my own inner compass.

- I choose to live my life in the present, with consciousness.

- I create Today as a celebration of my life.

- I Dance with a Light Heart.

- I Act with Bold Courage.

- I do not need anyone's permission to be my true self.

- Taking inspiration from the powerful vision of my future, I boldly set sail with courage and intent.

- I hold my course with focused attention and relentless commitment, as I weather the storms of life.

  *** There are more Positive Affirmations at the end of this book. ***

1 - Put Your Faith in Attitude, Not Circumstances

I set my own course through the ocean of life.
- Jonathan Lockwood Huie

From the way most people live, one would never guess that humans are beings of free will. Repetition can be a choice, but often it isn't.

The athlete or pianist who practices the same routine day after day, year after year, has their eye on a goal. The unending repetition is a conscious choice in the pursuit of a life dream. But what about the sameness of most lives?

Observe the morning commute, the after-work drink, the Sunday football game or religious service. How many of those people are consciously following their dream, training their mind, body, and spirit through that daily repetition? And how many are mindlessly slogging through each day out of habit and boredom?

You can take charge of your own life - today.

I set my own course through the ocean of life.
- Jonathan Lockwood Huie

2 - Choose Happiness

Happiness depends upon ourselves
- Aristotle

Happiness depends upon ourselves
- Aristotle

If you don't take full responsibility for your own happiness, who do you suppose will? Your happiness is a one person job - it begins and ends with you.

Consider the people in your life... which of them brighten your days? Chances are that the people you most enjoy are the people who have made their own choice to be happy in the face of their circumstances.

Everything you do or do not do in life is a choice. There is never anything you ever "need" to do. Every action and thought is a choice and has consequences - pleasant or unpleasant. Whether you go to work today, change jobs, smile at the bank teller, yell at your kids, complain about life, hold a daily celebration of gratitude for life - they are all choices. Happiness is a choice. Stay alert and make your conscious choices for happiness.

We all want to be happy, but something always gets in the way. There is never enough time... or money. Somebody is always failing to do what they are "supposed" to do... or not do. Our boss, our spouse, our kids, our parents, our friends, government, big business... "They" aren't doing it right. "They" failed us. We are angry, and we have a right to be angry. But is that righteous anger making us happy?

Happiness is not something anyone else can give us... or take away from us. Happiness is what we make of our lives... or don't. Whatever your circumstances, you can create a joyful life... or a miserable life. It is up to you.

3 - Accept that the World is Exactly as it Should be

The world is perfect. It's a mess. It has always been a mess. We are not going to change it. Our job is to straighten out our own lives.
- Joseph Campbell

What does Joseph Campbell mean by saying that the world is a mess and also that it is perfect?

I cannot know what was in Joseph Campbell's mind, but my interpretation of his statement is that the world is "perfect" because it exists exactly the way it does. If one believes in a benevolent and omnipotent God, the world is perfect because God created it exactly the way He did. If one is a humanist, the world is perfect simply because it is futile to wish for it be different - and such wishing causes suffering.

Here is another quote that says perhaps the same thing in a different way:

The world is perfect.
As you question your mind, this becomes more and more obvious.
Mind changes, and as a result, the world changes.
A clear mind heals everything that needs to be healed.
It can never be fooled into believing that there is one speck out of order.
- Byron Katie

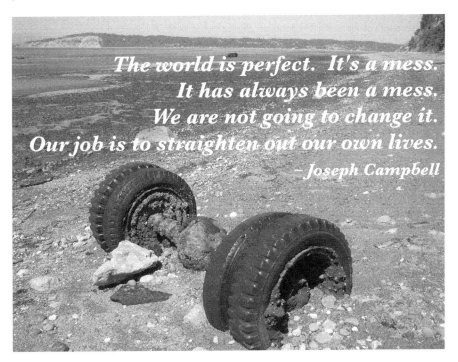

4 - Persevere - Happiness is Not Always an Easy Choice

Joy is a Choice - but it isn't an easy choice.

Of course you want to be happy, but life is hard. Your job's a pain, your family nags, and sometimes your body hurts, so how can a Joyful Life be a choice? It isn't an easy choice, but happiness *is* a choice that you can make.

Some choices are easy, because clearly defined alternatives are available. Choosing between vanilla and chocolate ice cream is such a choice. Other choices sometimes don't even appear to be choices.

If I live in Detroit, but I would prefer to live in Florida, I may not feel that I can choose to relocate. In reality, I always have a choice about where I live. I have my story about how my job, my house, my family, and my friends prevent me from moving, but it is truly only a story.

The greatest obstacle to a Joyful Life is your "story" about your life. Your story is filled with needs and obligations. You are sure that you "need" at least a certain income to live - and you likely feel that you "need" more money than you have. You "need" a "good" job. You "need" a big house. You feel obligated to do whatever your boss and your spouse ask of you. Perhaps you also feel obligated to serve your parents, children, friends, church, and more. STOP!

It's YOUR time - it's YOUR life - YOU get to choose how you use it. There is no way that your life is "supposed" to be. Your parents had their vision for your life. Your boss, your spouse, your church, your friends, and even the family next door have their ideas of how you should live your life. What about YOUR vision for your life? What do YOU want? YES, it matters what you want. YES you can have what you want.

CHOOSE the life you want, and CHOOSE to live Joyfully.

5 - Continue to Choose Happiness, Even When You Falter

Patience, persistence, and perseverance.
A little more each day, a little better each day.

When happiness appears unattainable, people begin to move through life in a sort of fog - unhappy, helpless to address the unhappiness, and unhappy about the helpless feeling.

There are two steps to take when life begins to blend into an unending fog, the first of the mind, the second of the heart.

Have a talk with your mind (it really is something separate from yourself). Lay down the law. "My life begins TODAY. I am like a newborn. I have what I have today; I have my fingers, my toes, some people in my life, some material and financial state. Yesterday is only a dream - perhaps a nightmare, perhaps a cherished memory, but only a dream - nothing more. I will make all decisions and actions based solely on what I have today as a starting point."

Personalize your conversation with your mind and be clear that you just won't tolerate any thoughts or actions that are not based on today's facts.

Moving to your heart, Breathe. Close your eyes and breathe deeply - slowly - fill your lungs with love and gratitude - exhale each and every trouble - again and again - gratitude in, troubles out.

Speak to your self from your heart as you would to a newborn baby, "I love you because I love you. You are a part of me, and I need no reasons to love you. Whether you cry or you smile, I love you. When you spill your milk or burp, there is nothing to forgive, there is no fault. You are love, I am love, and we are love."

6 - Give the Gift of Happiness to Your Friends and Family

The purpose of our lives is to be happy.
- Tenzin Gyatso, the 14th Dalai Lama

Your greatest gift to others is to be happy and to radiate your happiness to the entire world.

Choosing to live a happy life is not only our greatest gift to ourselves, it is also the greatest gift we can give to those around us. When we are happy, we radiate happiness, and that is infectious. Consider giving the gift of happiness to yourself as being your gift to all humanity.

Beyond being the greatest gift that you can give yourself, your choice to be happy is a magnificent present to your family, friends, and everyone you meet.

painting by Suze Stewart

7 - Honor Yourself

Self-respect is not a function of size, age, or wealth. Breathe deep, sing loud and sweet, "I am me, I am unique, I am magnificent."

Remember what the flight attendant says, "Put your own oxygen mask on first." You are of no use to anyone else if you have not taken care of your own needs first - this includes your own emotional, as well as physical, well-being.

Conformity is the jailer of freedom and the enemy of growth.
 - John F. Kennedy

Be yourself. There is nothing more for you to do than to be the best YOU that you can - no imitation, no pretense, no guilt, no shame.

Your #1 responsibility in life is to yourself. Lower your stress and raise your joy by focusing on yourself. Today and every day, take time to celebrate your life - whether an hour's meditation in a quiet natural space, or a brief moment's conscious pause to breathe deeply and celebrate gratitude for your life.

Advice is what we ask for when we already know the answer but wish we didn't.
 - Erica Jong

Trust yourself. Only you can live your life. Only you can taste your victories. Only you can suffer the sting of your defeats. Make your own choices, and accept your own consequences - for better or worse.

Self-respect is not a function of size, age, or wealth. Breathe deep, sing loud and sweet, "I am me, I am unique, I am magnificent."
 -Jonathan Lockwood Huie

If you don't love and respect yourself, who will? It all starts right here with ME. If I think that I'm a pretty good person, it doesn't much matter what anyone else thinks. And the irony is that once I like myself, most everyone else will like me too. People enjoy being around people who speak well of themselves - not in an arrogant boastful way, but with honest self-appreciation.

8 - Adopt these Affirmations for a Life You Love

1. I'm OK
2. I've Always Been OK
3. I Like Myself
4. I Think For Myself
5. I Have a Great Future
6. I Can Do Anything - Starting Right Now
7. I Play with Life and Have Fun
8. I Thank God

1. I'm OK - I'm alive and I have myself. My happiness does not depend on owning things, having money, or pleasing other people.

2. I've Always Been OK - Whenever I have been unhappy, it was because I blamed someone else, or myself, for something that happened. As soon as I stop blaming, and start forgiving everyone - others and myself - for everything, I begin to feel better about my past.

3. I Like Myself - I always do my best. Sometimes my best doesn't seem to be good enough, and I feel angry or afraid, or seem to have failed at what I tried. That's okay. My best is always good enough. I'm proud of myself and I like myself.

4. I Think For Myself - I CHOOSE to lead a happier life by gathering all the facts and making my own decisions. I choose NOT to "follow the crowd," and I choose NOT to just do what my friends do without thinking for myself.

5. I Have a Great Future - I welcome God into my mind and into my dreams. Whatever future I believe in, I can have, with God on my side.

6. I Can Do Anything - Starting Right Now. I have my dream, I have God, and I choose to move in the direction of my goal, even when I am afraid or unsure. Whenever I fall, I stand up, brush myself off, and keep moving toward my goal.

7. I Play with Life and Have Fun - Life is like a party game. The rules of the game of life have never been clear, and they keep changing during the game. Forget winning or losing, and just have fun.

8. I Thank God - I give thanks to God for everything, and I trust God with my life.

9 - Design Your Own Daily Affirmation

Designing your own daily affirmation may seem to be daunting, but give it a try anyway. Write your own affirmation about your abilities and your intentions. Repeat it each day before you leave your home. Start with the following, then modify it and add to it until it fully expresses your commitments, beliefs, and intents.

I am unlimited.
I take responsibility for my life.
My every action is a conscious choice.
I can accomplish anything good that I truly set my mind on.
I keep focus, and persevere.

10 - Know Where Your Path Leads

Faith is taking the first step even when you don't see the whole staircase.
- Martin Luther King, Jr.

Where are you going? Where does your path lead? You can never know the future, yet wandering aimlessly is unlikely to be the source of a fulfilling life.

Visualize being lost in the woods. You don't know where the path leads, you don't know what rivers, pitfalls, or wild animals lie ahead, but you can see the sun and stars, you can see the mountains sparkling in the distance. Life is like that, keep one eye on those shining mountains, and one on the path you follow.

Begin at the End. You can never reach your destination if you don't have a destination. Decide what accomplishments you want recorded on your tombstone. Take a whole quiet day to consider your life.

Be very clear that your happiness does NOT depend on reaching your goal. In fact, it's the reverse. Your happiness depends on accepting whatever life throws at you while you walk the path toward your goal. What is important for your happiness is having a goal, and working toward it.

Life is a journey - enjoy the journey

There is nowhere you have to reach. There is no destination, there is only the path (Life). Wherever you step, the path is under your feet. Whether you walk quickly or slowly, turn left or right, worry or relax, there is still no destination, and you are still walking the path.

You always have the ability to choose joy. Enjoy your journey.

11 - Choose the Purpose of Your Life

Life is without meaning. You bring the meaning to it. The meaning of life is whatever you ascribe it to be. Being alive is the meaning.
 - Joseph Campbell

This does NOT mean that life is meaningless or empty. Campbell's point is that we get to CHOOSE the meaning for our lives. Our lives mean exactly what we say they do - no more, no less. Each of us chooses their path in life.

You do not need anyone's permission to be your true self.

NO ONE has been granted the authority to tell me how my life should be lived. I answer only to myself and to Spirit - whatever that means to me.

Life is either a daring adventure or nothing.
 - Helen Keller

Why live? Adding one to my count of days, or postponing a feared death by another day do not inspire me. I live to experience something new each day - to learn something new, meet a new friend, bring joy into someone's life, feel the wind newly on my skin, touch a new fear, a new anger, and with focused intent and good fortune, find an ample measure of my own joy.

The meaning of Life is whatever we Choose.

We give life its meaning. See life as ugly and painful if you choose, or see it as beautiful and joyful. There is no inherent meaning in life. You give life its meaning. It's your Choice.

Life is either a daring adventure or nothing.
 - Helen Keller

12 - Take Charge of Your Life

Say NO to the demands of the world.
Say YES to the longings of your own heart.

Do you ever stop to ask yourself WHY
you "need to do" something? What is
the "need," and on whose authority has
the need been established?

*We disrespect ourselves and our free-will
whenever we say that we NEED TO DO
something.*

Everything we do is a choice! In every
instant, we are making a choice about
what we will do in that instant (as well
as a choice about what we will think in
that instant).

We may choose to turn off and shut
down our conscious attention, and
allow the autopilot of our habits and
instincts to make our choices, but they
are still choices.

There is nothing I ever need to have.
There is nothing I ever need to do.

I Say NO to the demands of the world.
I Say YES to the longings of my own heart.

- Jonathan Lockwood Huie

I have no need to conform to the stereotypes others have defined for me

Your spouse says "You need to go to the grocery store today," and you say "I need
to go to the grocery store today," or perhaps you say to yourself "I need to get a
divorce." Look at all the "need to's." Who says so? There is no inherent "should,"
"must," or "need to" here. There are choices and there are consequences. The
consequence of not going to the grocery store today may be eating peanut butter
sandwiches or sleeping alone tonight, but there is no "need to."

13 - Hold No Expectations of Life

Life will not meet your expectations - choose joy anyway

When we have expectations, we KNOW how people SHOULD behave, and we can have no compassion. Once we accept that there is a uniquely "right" path for each of us, we can be compassionate.

Mostly, it is human to dislike surprises - often with great intensity. Be open to new ways; sometimes newness just knocks on our door; welcome it.

It is nearly a certainty that some of your expectations will not be met today - choose Joy anyway.

Each of us is burdened by an unlimited number of expectations (demands) that we hold for the actions of others. We know that there is a right way to do things, and are often outraged when our expectations are not met.

Usually, we are unaware that we merely have a strong opinion and point-of-view. We are sure that we know how everything is supposed to be, but virtually everything that we KNOW to be true is only true from our own perspective.

It ain't what you don't know that gets you into trouble. It's what you know for sure that just ain't so. - Mark Twain

It ain't what you don't know that gets you into trouble. It's what you know for sure that just ain't so. - Mark Twain

14 - Welcome the Unexpected

Compassion blooms where there is no expectation.

The following is one of the many times when my subconscious expectations have been shattered...

Several years ago on a trip to Tibet, I visited a mountainside Buddhist monastery nestled in the spectacularly beautiful vista far beyond the bustle of urban Lhasa.

As the older vehicle which passed for a bus struggled up the mountain switchbacks, distant views of the monastery repeatedly flashed into my view and then immediately clicked off as we twisted and turned. Finally, we neared our goal, and slowly approached.

I was excited and joyful to be visiting this highly revered sanctuary, as my already deep appreciation of Buddhist monks had been heightened by my experience in a Lhasa monastery, where I was nearly brought to tears by the overwhelming presence of five hundred deeply resonate voices chanting their passionate connection to humanity and to the infinite. I could still feel their commitment and compassion resonating through my bones.

As we exited the bus and started walking toward the rural monastery, I was captivated by the crisp cool air, the stark blue of the cloudless sky, and the splendor of the mountains. I moved away from the group and walked to the edge of the plateau to get a better view of the vista. Above, the intense sun punctuating the clear sky; to the right, a landscape of drought-resistant plants and dwarf trees; across the canyon, a couple of mountain goats foraging peacefully; and below... the most immense pile of trash and garbage I have ever seen.

I have seen the urban garbage heaps that are euphemistically called "land fills." This small monastery's heap fully matched a small city's repository in size, and the noxious smells wafting from the canyon surpassed those of most any urban landfill. There were bottles, there were Coke cans, there were rusted remnants of ancient machinery, and there was garbage - today's garbage, yesterday's garbage, rotted garbage, and very rotted garbage - with no attempt whatsoever to cover it, compost it, deodorize it, or camouflage it in any way.

In a split second, my assumptions and expectations shattered like a stack of plates dropped by a stumbling waiter.

Buddhist monks weren't SUPPOSED to do this! These were the people who revered all life - the people who wouldn't step on an ant. These were the people who meticulously preserved manuscripts for thousands of years. These were the people whose every day was scheduled to the minute.

After a few minutes I realized that the giant garbage heap was actually very logical. These monks were focused on the divine and on compassion for all beings; they had little concern for the affairs of the world. In my value system, "natural beauty" held a place of honor; in theirs it did not.

Exercise: Think of a time when your assumptions and expectations about something or someone were shattered. Was the experience devastating or educational? Imagine the power of seeking out some of your assumptions and expectations and intentionally blowing them up.

Welcome the Unexpected.

Most people think of surprises as being something unpleasant. Consider moving past this instinctive fear of the unknown and welcoming the unexpected.

15 - Make Conscious Choices About What and Who to Trust

Stay Conscious and Aware - Do not decide who to trust, decide which ideas to trust.

What or who do you trust, or depend upon? Most of the time it is not obvious where we are placing our trust. Every time you drive down the highway, you are trusting thousands of people to stay in their own lane, stop at red lights, keep to the right of oncoming traffic (in the United States), and follow a myriad of other conventions.

Perhaps you trust your doctor, your lawyer, your boss - perhaps not. Perhaps you trust in a "Higher Power" - perhaps you don't. Trust is something that we may become aware of when we fly in an airplane, and certainly wonder about if we parachute or bungee jump, but most of the time, we become oblivious to the trust we have, or don't have.

Exercise: Take time today, and often, to consciously examine what and who you trust. Especially focus on WHY you do or do not trust something or someone.

Blind trust is a bad habit - conscious trust is one of the underpinnings of a great life.

16 - Say NO to Stress

I will not be governed by the tyranny of immediacy.
- Mary Anne Radmacher

They don't call them DEADlines for nothing - keep breathing.

Stress is to your emotional health as junk food is to your physical health. You need a certain amount of food to sustain your life, but overeating and eating the wrong foods are unhealthy and sometimes dangerous.

As you need food to live, you also need a certain amount of emotional stimulation, but unless you choose to live alone far from the reaches of civilization, you are bombarded daily with innumerable stressors (agents, conditions, or other stimuli that cause stress). You hear the daily woes of friends and family. Your job and your daily commute are filled with agitation. Just a few minutes of the 11 o'clock news provides far more than your daily requirement of emotional stimulation.

What to do?

Ask yourself what is the worst that can happen: Usually the worst isn't really so bad. For example, the worst your boss can ever do is to fire you, and if you hate your job, that would be a blessing in disguise.

17 - Make No Demands of Life

The more you expect, the more you get disappointed in life.
- Anonymous

Be clear that expectations are demands. Demanding that life turn out the way we prefer is a sure path to disappointment and suffering. Happiness lies in having no expectations, and accepting life as it comes.

God grant me the serenity
To accept the things I cannot change;
Courage to change the things I can;
And wisdom to know the difference.
- Reinhold Niebuhr

You ask someone to do something, they don't do it, and you get upset - raising your stress level. Suppose you asked less of other people? Your stress level would go way down. For example, you want your teenagers to keep their rooms tidy. For them, a structured living space is not a priority. Ask yourself whether exerting your control is worth the high stress level that it causes you.

True happiness begins when I choose to accept and love all of life.

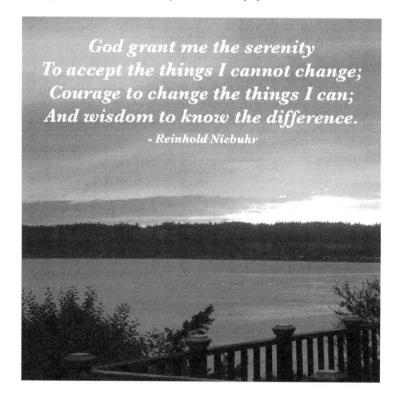

18 - Be Prepared

Success consists of going from failure to failure without loss of enthusiasm.
- Winston Churchill

The only thing we have to fear is fear itself.
- Franklin D. Roosevelt

Mentally, prepare for failures: Your boss WILL be critical of your work. Your cell phone and computer WILL fail. The stock market WILL drop. There WILL be another terrorist attack or war. It is just life. If you are mentally prepared, you won't be surprised or get stressed when the inevitable happens.

What about being prepared physically? Yes, keep a first aid kit and fire extinguisher handy. Yes, keep a stock of food and bottled water in your house. Yes, plan where you would reunite with your family after a disaster. But remember that there are two reasons for making these preparations. Not only are the supplies and plans likely to be helpful, but more importantly, having taken those actions aids you in relaxing and not worrying about the future.

Know that the unexpected will happen and that worrying about what might happen in the future can only destroy your happiness today. Enjoy today.

Success is failure recycled. Life is death reborn.

- Jonathan Lockwood Huie

19 - Never Doubt the Power of Your Intent

As many raindrops join to form a great river of water, many souls join their highest intent to form the river of evolved consciousness.

Intent (or intention) is an amazingly powerful force. Your intent can shift your whole world. The intent of a few thousand can shift the whole world for all humanity. Never doubt the power of your intent.

Stay Alert, and doors will open.

You can never know when and where a magic door will open for you, so pay attention, stay watchful, and never give up hope.

20 - Feel Your Connection With the Infinite (a meditation)

I Am One With Spirit and All Creation - I give thanks for the unity of all creation and for everything that has brought me to this moment. I release my entire being to the gentle nurture of Spirit.

Whenever it appears that life's troubles are conspiring against me, I find great comfort in this simple meditation...

Choose a quiet place and sit comfortably but erect in a chair with no arms. Remove your glasses, watch, jewelry and metal objects.

Place your feet flat on the floor. Lift your arms off your lap and extend them slightly to the side.

Close your eyes and begin to breathe deeply and rhythmically. Keeping your eyes shut, raise your chin slightly and focus your inner gaze upward.

With each in-breath, visualize clean white energy streaming in through the top of your head. Feel the renewal, the strength, the connection with Spirit and all creation. Feel the wellbeing, the relaxation, the sense of peace. Let the corners of your mouth form just the slightest smile of contentment in the knowing that all is right with your world.

On each out-breath, visualize dark clouds of stale energy leaving from the soles of your feet. Feel the tensions, the angers, the frustrations draining from your body. Feel all your fears and stress falling away as the dark cloud drifts toward the center of the earth.

As you continue breathing slowly, in and out, visualizing the new energy entering and the old energy leaving, the energy leaving through the soles of your feet will grow lighter, changing from black to dark gray to a lighter gray.

When the color of the energy you are exhaling has become almost as bright as the clean new energy that you are breathing in through the crown of your head, the process is complete.

Feel renewed and at peace with Spirit, with the world, with all people and beings, with yourself, with your past, your present and your future.

Give thanks for all that ever has been, all that is, and all that ever will be.

21 - Tame Unhealthy Habits

By nature, we are all creatures of habit. We instinctively adopt familiar routines for most activities.

As fish are unaware of water because they have never known anything else, so too, we are unaware of our habits until we discover alternatives.

While we may have some habits, like smoking, that we recognize as habits, we also have many habits of which we are completely unaware. Many of the opinions we hold are rooted in habitual thinking, rather than in careful analysis.

Consider making an on-going practice of questioning all your repetitive behaviors. Perhaps some of them are habits you would like to break.

We eat about the same number of meals each day - at more or less the same times. We have a regular pattern of sleeping - unless it is perturbed by illness or shift work. Most everything we do is habitual.

You probably eat three meals each day, but why? Why not two or five? There is nothing particularly "natural" about our pattern of eating three meals each day - it is just a habit that we share with most of those around us. Actually, a number of studies indicate that eating five smaller meals is more satisfying and healthier than eating three large ones.

You will always have habits - things you do regularly and without conscious thought - but you do have the ability to CHOOSE your habits. Here's how...

1. Begin to pay attention to WHAT you do, WHEN you do it, and WHY you do it. One of the bad habits I fell into was eating a large dish of ice cream in the late evening. Obviously, "ice cream" was the "what," but the "when" was more than just "in the evening." "When" was times I felt stressed, hadn't had a satisfying dinner, or was bored. "Why" was mouth sensation, having something to do with my hands, and sometimes hunger.

2. Keep a journal of the "what", "when," and "why." Make an entry whenever you find yourself doing something that isn't really your choice. You will find that you gain better insight into the "when's" and "why's" as you get more entries in your journal. Soon a pattern will emerge that can enable you to find healthy habits to replace the harmful ones.

3. Look for other activities that would satisfy the "when" and "why." A hot bath for stress, hard candy for mouth sensation, a good book for activity, a warm bowl of soup for real hunger.

4. Make the undesirable activity difficult. Don't keep the cigarettes or ice cream in the house. When ice cream was in my own freezer, it was hard to resist, but when eating a dish of super chocolate chunk required a trip to the convenience store, it was much easier to turn my attention to other activities and a low calorie snack - if any snack at all.

5. Begin new habits not only because you need them to replace unhealthy ones, but also because they are the things you always wanted to do, but couldn't find the time or money. That book club or yoga class makes a great substitute for the eating or smoking, and you can more than pay for your health club membership with what you save on cigarettes.

22 - De-Stress at Work

To reduce the effects of stress in the workplace, take an emotional and spiritual, as well as a physical break, at least every two hours, preferably every hour.

Here are five de-stressors you can do in thirty seconds each...

1. Stretch your hands, arms, and shoulders. In addition to unwinding the kinks, this exercise provides a good warm-up for any of the other emotional exercises. Stand and hold your arms out to your sides so your body and arms form a cross. Gently bend each hand back at the wrist until the fingers point straight upward. Keeping your arms fully extended to the sides, with your fingers still extended upward, twist each hand and arm in a wringing motion as if you were operating a screwdriver.

2. Conscious Breathing: Breathe deeply and slowly. Focus your entire attention on each in-breath and out-breath. Visualize drawing new clean energy in through the top of your head on each in-breath, and expelling old stale energy out the soles of your feet on each out-breath.

3. Inner Smile: While conscious breathing, close your eyes and set the corners of your mouth in just the slightest smile. Visualize your smile growing larger and larger, and your happiness increasing.

4. Release your burdens: One by one, focus on each memory or fear that troubles you, hold it close, then release it back to the Universe. Release each incident from your past that still bothers you. Release each fear - your fears about your health, your family, your job, and every other fear. Breathe deeply, and give thanks.

5. Merging: While conscious breathing, close your eyes and visualize merging with the entire Universe - with each person, each animal, each plant, each bit of everything seen and unseen. Feel a unity with Spirit and all that is.

23 - Cool Your Anger - Use Love to Conquer Hate

Hate is never conquered by hate,
Hate is only conquered by love.
- The Buddha

Where there is no accusation of "fault," there can be no anger.

When I get angry, I am always angry AT someone - perhaps my friend or spouse, perhaps a stranger, perhaps the nameless "they" - "those people at the bank wronged me," perhaps God, or perhaps myself. In any case, when I get angry, I want to find someone to be "responsible" for what happened.

My window breaks. I want to know WHO broke my window. Who threw the rock, or who built the defective

Hate is never conquered by hate,
Hate is only conquered by love.
- the Buddha

window, or who didn't prevent the hurricane or meteorite. America's penchant for filing law suits, along with untold misery, is built upon pandering to our instinct to blame someone whenever life doesn't occur as we prefer.

Life just happens - enjoy it anyway.

Anger is something that each one of us has experienced - some of us only occasionally, some almost daily. Can we eliminate all anger? Probably not. We will always have expectations, and those expectations will often be unmet.

Disappointment is the principle cause of anger. When we are disappointed, we look for someone to blame. Declaring someone to be at fault is the nature of anger. Anger is always directed at someone - possibly God or the non-specific *they*, but at *some* animate entity.

When you begin to feel angry, choose not to find fault. If you find yourself angry at someone close to you, focus on what you love about them. If you start to get angry at a stranger, call upon your commitment to love all humanity. For specific techniques to stop anger, read the next "secret" *Stop Anger Before It Stops You.*

24 - Stop Anger Before It Stops You

Being angry is as close as a human being can come to experiencing hell on earth.

You've told yourself a hundred times that you aren't going to get angry - really angry - ever again, but wham, you start to feel that telltale heat, locked shoulders, clenched jaw, shallow breathing. Someone has just done something really awful and you are angry at them. What now?

Try these techniques to stop anger before it stops you…

1. Recognize when you are angry: It may not immediately occur to you that you are angry. You know that you have been wronged, and you can see everyone around you take a step back, but especially if you are really angry, it may take a while to gain the clarity to acknowledge your anger. Anger clouds perception and thinking, so make a special effort to spot it early and put it into words, "I am angry."

2. Breathe deeply: Concentrate on taking slow deep breaths. Sometimes this is all it takes to break out of anger and gain clarity on the issue. At other times, breathing deeply is just a beginning, but it paves the way for the rest of the secrets.

3. Focus your anger: Get clear what you are angry about and who you are angry at. Talk to yourself, "I am angry at Joe because he ..." Don't let your anger expand onto innocent bystanders, especially those trying to help calm you down. Don't refocus your anger onto everything that Joe has ever done or failed to do.

4. Remember that you are in charge: Anger is an expression of frustration and helplessness. Remember that you always have options - you can design your own life. No one can steal your happiness - unless you let them.

5. Look for the silver lining: There is a silver lining to every disappointment. Your boss fired you and you are furious. Probably it was a blessing. Now you have the opportunity to get a better job that you really enjoy.

6. Consider forgiveness: Angry and happy don't mix. Flush out the angry, and the happy has a place to put down roots. Forgive everyone for everything in order to give anger and resentment a chance to fade. Forgive and you can become happy. Forgiving is not a gift to someone else - Forgiving is our gift to ourselves - a great gift - the gift of happiness.

7. Accept that Life is NOT "Supposed to be Fair": Know that there is no single way that life is "supposed" to be. Demanding that life meet our expectations is a sure fire recipe for a miserable existence. Life is a game with no rules. Life just happens to us regardless of our best intentions. To choose happiness, be open to receiving whatever life throws at you - with Gratitude. Have NO Expectations of life.

25 - Never Let Anyone Get Your Goat

Stay Happy, Never Let Anyone Get Your Goat, Push Your Buttons, Get You Riled Up, or Annoy You

Whether phrased as "push your buttons," "get your goat," "get you riled up," or "annoy you," it's no fun to be on the receiving end. How to cope?

1. Don't take it personally. Even when someone criticizes your actions or demeans your very nature, know that they are merely directing their inner turmoil in your direction. Someone else's opinion of you is mostly irrelevant, and basically none of your business. Don't assume that there is any validity to an accusation. Perhaps there is a valuable lesson buried inside the unkindness that merits objective consideration, but negative emotions are best just quickly discarded.

2. Look to the positive people in your life for support. If you balance many positive and supportive friends against one or two negative influences, it is much easier to cope. If you don't currently have enough positive people in your life, begin a focused effort to add positive people to your inner circle. If you don't have personal connections, search for groups of positive people at MeetUp.com

3. Remove negative people from your life. Yes you can, even if it's your boss. You don't need that job so much that it's worth your health or happiness. Everything in life is a choice. Sometimes making a change is important, while other times just knowing that you hold the power to make a different choice is enough.

4. Forgive the offender, not for their sake, but for your own sake. The act of forgiving releases your anger and provides space for rational thinking and action.

5. Be grateful for the wake-up call. Any time that someone or something grabs your attention is a good time to be grateful - even if the message is unpleasant. Something is happening that requires your conscious awareness. Perhaps you have a lesson to learn or an action to take. Perhaps it is time to remove another negative influence from your life.

6. Release any expectations that the unkind person should have acted differently. Life is not fair, and you only cause yourself unhappiness if you hold an expectation that life or any individual should be fair or kind.

26 - Be Warned: (d)ANGER spells DANGER

Anger and Danger are intimately intertwined. An angry person is a dangerous person, whether that person crosses our path or whether the angry person is our own self. To complete the anger/danger cycle, whenever we feel threatened - when we believe we are in danger - we tend to exhibit anger as well as fear. We look for someone to blame for the dangerous situation, and direct our anger toward them.

Being angry is as close as a human being can come to experiencing hell on earth.

Angry? Pause. Breathe deeply. Step back and look at the issue from a new perspective.

Anger? perhaps there is a better way.

Know that anger is always fear and frustration. What if we could lean back into the arms of Spirit and trust the future? What if...

(d)ANGER spells DANGER

- Jonathan Lockwood Huie

27 - Summon the Courage to Act in the Face of Fear.

Courage is resistance to fear, mastery of fear - not absence of fear.
- Mark Twain

I am a human being - so I feel fear - it's that simple. All human beings are afraid - from time to time. Some more than others - some more intensely than others. Fear is related to circumstance. We can never be totally without fear, but we can learn to deal with our fear. The road to a life you love is not without fear - it is managing your fear - living with your fear - being at peace with your fear.

Cold Gripping Fear

They don't call it cold gripping fear for nothing. It's that scared, panicked, apprehensive, afraid, you name it feeling that hits everywhere at once - tightened shoulders, knotted stomach, shivery cold. When the body sensations get the upper hand, observe them and give thanks to your body for reminding you that you are fully human. Take a deep breath - feel gratitude - life is good - the breath is healing - take comfort - breathe deeply - mmmm... You are still here and through the eye of the needle.

The chills fade, the shoulders loosen, the stomach unknots, and digestion returns. Whatever may happen in the future, today is a good day.

Virtually all humans can recall the experience of cold gripping fear - and the others have short memories. What is that cramp in your stomach, the knot in the shoulders, the cold and shivers? It's the fight-or-flight reaction shutting down your digestive tract and other functions that can be deferred, and it has been with the human race from the very beginning. It's getting your body ready to either fight or run away from that saber-toothed tiger.

Our body is doing just what it's supposed to have done for the last million years. If our body hadn't worked that way, saber-toothed tigers would have been better fed, and *homo sapiens* would be a dead end branch on the evolutionary tree. Those early humans whose biochemistries were tuned to universal love and acceptance became lunch for the tiger, or a trophy head for the neighboring tribe, and didn't pass any of their genes down to us.

So let's thank our fight-or-flight physiologies for having gotten us this far. We can't wish away the physicality of our humanity no matter how hard we try, so let's love our bodies, and our genetics, and our ancestors.

Accepting that our physical fear is an inherently human quality is the first step toward leading a courageous and joyful life. To be courageous is *not* to be without fear - to be courageous is to accept our fear and to act in the face of it.

Once we act in the face of fear, our fear starts to dissipate. Our fear stops having center stage, and starts to shrivel up. Those things on which we focus our attention get stronger, and those things that lose our attention grow weaker. So it is with fear. Once we place our attention on more important things, fear shrivels.

To Remember: Whenever you observe physical sensations of fear in your body - whether Cold Gripping Fear, or just a twinge of what might be called apprehension or concern - just observe your physical reactions. Don't judge your physical reactions as being bad - they are just physical reactions. Thank your fear - give thanks to your body for reminding you that you're human. Take a deep breath - express gratitude - remember the overarching goodness of life - take another healing breath - feel comforted by Spirit - breathe deeply - exhale mmmm... and give thanks for everything that has brought you to this moment.

Nothing in life is to be feared,
it is only to be understood.
Now is the time to understand
more, so that we may fear less.
- Marie Curie (scientist 1867-1934)

28 - Manage Overwhelm

Life only appears to be rushing toward us

"Oh my God!" we scream as our fragile serenity is overwhelmed by the impending vagaries of LIFE appearing as an unleashed Niagara Falls bearing down upon us.

Life only appears to be rushing toward us
- *Jonathan Lockwood Huie*

What if it were only an illusion? Perhaps life is not as threatening as it appears. Perhaps the greatest threat to our serenity is our fear of the future - our fear of the unknown. Perhaps, as Franklin D. Roosevelt said, *The Only Thing We Have to Fear Is Fear Itself.*

"Concern" is a natural emotion for humans, but we can minimize our suffering by recognizing the nature of our concerns, and by consciously focusing our attention on our gratitude for the Joys of our life.

To Remember: Whenever you recognize that you are experiencing a concern, question what you are really afraid of - being very specific, and continuing to look more deeply. Ask yourself what is the worst possible outcome and whether you could survive that. Then question whether you choose to continue to devote time and energy to the concern. Is this concern worth suffering over - perhaps even to the degree of impacting your physical health?

Consciously going through this process works. It is very different from just trying to tell yourself "calm down, don't worry, everything's okay." The intermediate steps of specifically identifying the lowest level, most basic fears and possible consequences are what make this process work. Try it.

29 - Learn To Cope With Loss, Grief and Fear Of Death

It is not death or pain that is to be dreaded, but the fear of pain or death.
 - Epictetus

There is no death, only a change of worlds.
 - Chief Seattle

Do not mourn the dead, but comfort the living.

Here are the pillars that support me as I confront the specter of death. For me, these affirmations proclaim the joy and purpose of life. May they also serve you well.

1. Life is what I make of it. Whether I have hours or decades remaining, I can choose to focus on living a happy and compassionate life - unencumbered by fears of future dangers, including death.

2. Once someone has "passed on," they are no longer suffering. Whether or not I believe that they are now "in a better place," I can be sure that they are no longer suffering. While, I certainly feel compassion for the grief and loss of the departed one's family and friends, my sympathy is for the living, not the dead.

3. Whenever I die, my life will be complete and a finished work. If I believe that the purpose of my life is preordained by a higher power, it is logical to believe that my life is also preordained to fulfill that purpose - however much time I am on this earth. However, if I believe that I have free-will, the only demand upon my earthly time is that I do my best - whatever the result.

4. I choose to overcome my instinctive fear of the unknown. All humans naturally fear the unknown. I will fight that fear every day - and I will win. In winning my battle with fear, I win my freedom and my happiness.

5. I am one with Spirit - Spirit is my strength. Whatever the details of my beliefs, and however I choose to commune with my Higher Power, it is my rock and my Pillar of Life.

30 - Avoid Urgency - Nothing is *That* Important

Nature does not hurry, yet everything is accomplished.
- Lao Tzu

"Hurry up" ranks right up there with "you need to" as a destroyer of our humanity.

Why hurry? Why the urgency? What is the worst that could happen if you didn't meet someone's deadline? Is a deadline worth your health and happiness? Consider a gentler, quieter, slower life. Pause to smell the roses, to breathe, to take quiet moments for yourself.

Hurrying - urgency - robs life of its quality. Patience is more than a virtue, patience is a joyful way of living. Don't accomplish less, but focus on the most important things, and proceed at a natural comfortable pace. The soft water of the river cuts through the hardest rock - in its own time.

Time, like life itself, has no inherent meaning. We give our own meaning to time as to life.

Urgent? Why?

Time, like life itself, has no inherent meaning. We give our own meaning to time, as to life.
- Jonathan Lockwood Huie

31 - Live in the Present

Life is best when I wish neither to hurry the future nor to slow it.

TODAY is what life is all about. When I desire for the future to arrive quickly, I become unable to savor today. I can't live in tomorrow, and when I focus all my energies on the future, I shortchange today. Likewise, fearing the future emasculates today, leaving it dry and lifeless.

Keep your feet firmly planted on the ground as you reach for the stars.

Stop wishing and fearing the future long enough to be fully present in TODAY. Some great things are happening today that bear no resemblance to what you planned.

Suspended between earth and sky, my humanity draws from both, my tendrils reach for the energies of each. Spirit and Ground - equal yet opposite, the lightness and the solidarity, the ephemeral and the substantial. The substantial is no more and no less than the ephemeral, just different.

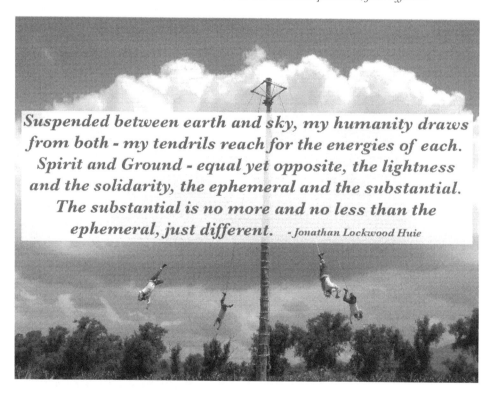

Suspended between earth and sky, my humanity draws from both - my tendrils reach for the energies of each. Spirit and Ground - equal yet opposite, the lightness and the solidarity, the ephemeral and the substantial. The substantial is no more and no less than the ephemeral, just different. - Jonathan Lockwood Huie

32 - Balance Living in the Now with Preparing for Tomorrow

Are you feeling stressed and upset? If so, you are worrying about tomorrow. Events that have already occurred may cause you regret, but they only appear to cause worry. If you just lost your job, you are not worrying about losing your job - that already happened. You are worrying about paying your bills and finding a new job. Those are worries about tomorrow.

Worrying is just a natural human emotion, and everyone worries, right? Actually not. Worry is a bad habit that most people acquire, and like all habits, can be broken.

When you worry about what may or may not occur in the future, you miss the joy that is available today - each and every day. So is the answer to focus only on today, and let tomorrow take care of itself? That sounds good - until tomorrow arrives and you are not prepared.

It's a paradox. How does one balance living in the now with preparing responsibly for the future? The key to this dilemma lies in the distinction between "worrying about the future," and "preparing for the future." The two concepts are not at all the same.

There are two aspects to preparing for the future. The one that is more familiar to most people is planning. You know the mortgage is due next week so you save the money - You know you want to fit into your clothes tomorrow, so you forgo that second helping. Planning for the future is fully compatible with living joyfully today.

The other aspect of preparing for the future is accepting that things will probably not turn out the way you plan. Creating this acceptance of life's uncertainties is much more challenging than formulating and following through on plans.

The source of most worry is a lack of acceptance of the uncertainties of the future. When one fully lives a life of acceptance, life's vagaries are not merely tolerated, but are enjoyed because they are life's gifts. If one is religiously inclined, whatever life delivers is a gift from the Creator. If one holds other beliefs, then whatever happens is just what there is to work with - so why not enjoy it.

The recipe for a joyful life is planning and preparing for the future, while simultaneously accepting that you hold virtually no control over future events. By placing no demands on the future, you can enjoy whatever it brings.

33 - See Each Day as a New Beginning

It is never too late to begin. - Anonymous

I Dream This Day of Wondrous Things,
of Peace and Hope and Pride.
I Dance My Dance with Life Today,
I'm Filled with Love Inside.

Today is a good day for everything you ever wanted to do but didn't believe you could. Choose something that has always seemed out of your reach, and begin today. Perhaps the smallest baby step today, and a slightly larger step tomorrow.

It is never too late to begin. Remember that you always wanted to play the piano, paint, write poetry, start a journal, read that challenging book, begin stargazing, learn a little Spanish, take up yoga or qigong, build something special. There will never be a better day to begin than today. Just do it.

Don't project your past onto your future. Suppose you won the lottery yesterday, would that mean you will win the lottery again tomorrow? Usually, we are fairly realistic about not expecting a run of good fortune to continue, but when we hit a streak of bad luck, we tend to project that failure into our future and think times will never get better. So you stepped on a banana peel and slipped yesterday, does that mean it will happen again tomorrow? If you got fired or your lover left, it's unfortunate, but there's always tomorrow - a tomorrow that can shine so long as you don't project yesterday's shadow upon it.

Another Sunrise, Another New Beginning
- Jonathan Lockwood Huie

34 - Allow Life be an Adventure of Discovery

Soar - it's your natural state.

Why settle for less? If you do not yet feel your wings spreading, look for the chains tethering you to your history. You were born wild and free. What happened? Are you willing to break with your past?

When you choose to move past fear - fear of failure, fear of embarrassment, fear of "looking bad," fear of losing

Soar, It's Your Natural State.
- Jonathan Lockwood Huie

respect - life becomes much lighter, and most any task becomes possible - perhaps even enjoyable. Most any challenge can become an adventure of discovery.

Choose what lies in the shadows to be a matter for discovery and adventure, rather than fear.
- Jonathan Lockwood Huie

Choose what lies in the shadows to be a matter for discovery and adventure, rather than fear.

We all have an instinctive fear of the unseen. Make a conscious effort to discover and embrace the unfamiliar - to view the unknown not as a lurking monster, but as a glorious adventure.

Life is a grand adventure - enjoy the ride.

Helen Keller said *Life is either a daring adventure or nothing.* Right on! Regardless of what we do or don't do, life is a dangerous and ultimately fatal undertaking, so don't hold back, play it safe, or only go halfway. Play full-out and enjoy all of Life.

None of us is perfect - and that's OK.

Life is not about perfection - or a quest for perfection. Life is about enjoying what we have - for as long as we have it.

35 - See Yourself As Others See You

He who knows others is wise. He who knows himself is enlightened.
- Lao Tzu

People only see what they are prepared to see.
- Ralph Waldo Emerson

It's a cozy little luncheon with the girls, or a "no holds barred" time with the guys. Everyone tells their story and complains a little. "My marriage is getting worse," "My boss doesn't appreciate me," "I don't know what to do next." Amazingly, everyone at that table knows just how to fix everyone's problems - except their own. Why?

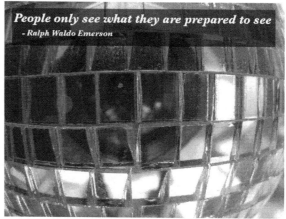

We are so close to our own issues that we see impossibility in each proposed solution. "I couldn't just leave my abusive spouse, I need the money and the house, I couldn't survive on my own." Really? We can tell a friend how to leave an unworkable job, marriage, or friendship, and a moment later recoil in horror when a similar suggestion is offered for our dilemma.

Take a deep breath. Step back from the situation to gain a clear perspective. Be courageous and bold. Consider carefully what advice you would give to a good friend who was in the same circumstances that trouble you, and then accept that advice and put it into action - today.

36 - Consider How You Want to be Remembered

How do you want to be remembered?
Live life full out - Begin today
- Jonathan Lockwood Huie

How do you want to be remembered? Live life full out - Begin today.

What do you want written on your tombstone? It won't be there if you haven't done it. Start today. If you want "never missed a day of work," go for it, but if you want it said that you were a good friend, a loving spouse and parent, or perhaps that you "radiated happiness to all around - put a smile on every face - inspired us all to be the best we could be," you might want to start today to lighten up, and begin to put happiness - yours, your family's, and your friends - ahead of material success or "achievement."

What you do TODAY is what others will remember. Make today count.

Follow Your Bliss. - Joseph Campbell

If you want to do it, do it - TODAY.

37 - Design Your Future

I am the call.
From far beyond this life,
I hear the call.
From place beyond all place,
I feel the call.
From time before all time,
I know the call.
From one before all ones,
I am the call.

We are called. We are all called. We are called from beyond all place and time, by a power beyond all power. When you close your eyes, let your shoulders sag, and spread your arms wide, you can feel the call. The call says "You are here for a reason. Your life is important."

The caller remains anonymous. We refrain from asking for a name. God? Our Ancestors? Gaia? Random biochemistry? Questions aside, focus on the message "There is a purpose to your life. Find your purpose."

Visualize being in the future you desire. Make that vision so real you can taste and smell it - a three-dimensional full-color motion picture with surround-sound. That is your goal - your destination. Never forget it - never lose track of it. Let what you do every day be done with that vision in mind. Be the aspiring athlete or musician whose every day moves them one inch closer to that three-minute mile or perfect concerto.

Design Your Future: Don't be a passive tumbleweed blown by the winds of life. Envision the future you want, and then take action to create that future. Often, you will fail. Plan again and take action again.

Powerful dreams inspire projects that can alter our world.

YOU make a difference to the world. Act on your dreams today.

38 - Speak Your Intention - It Will Be So

In the beginning was the Word.
  - John 1:1

What we think, we become. All that we are arises with our thoughts. With our thoughts, we make the world.
  - The Buddha

The Buddha is describing what we call *Intent* or *Intention*. We hold the power to make things happen through our intent - to the extent that we use our intention with compassion and without ego.

Is intent - or intention - real? While not scientifically provable, intent is certainly very real in my personal experience, and the experience of those of my community.

My Intent is my transmission to the entire Universe. It is the way I speak my vision for the future. While I can "speak" anything to the Universe, many transmissions are not received or are diverted.

My compassionate intents are generally received clearly and acted upon - perhaps not immediately, or in exactly the way I hope- but acted upon favorably, nonetheless.

However desires that are neutral - such as my desire to win the lottery - are just ignored. Further, my harmful or "evil" desires are not only rejected by the Universe, but are mirrored back to me as intense personal suffering - essentially Hell-on-earth.

The so-called "Law of Attraction" states that the Universe will give you *anything* you want. That is only half-true in that you can have anything that you request with compassion. The untruth is the expectation that the Universe will respond favorably when you ask for money or ask to harm others.

Consider the distinction between affluence and riches. Affluence is a state of mind. I can perceive affluence regardless of my external circumstances. The Universe responds favorably when I request affluence. I always receive the feeling of having everything I need. Sometimes I actually receive riches, and sometimes I receive that satisfied feeling with what the Universe deems is best for me. Either way, I truly receive affluence.

When you call upon your *Intention* or *Law of Attraction*, just remember that it will provide what you request with compassion, but not satisfy your hurtful or greedy requests.

39 - Create Good Endings - They Precede Good Beginnings

Celebrate endings - for they precede new beginnings.

Endings - sometimes a season of sorrow and grief. Endings - what must precede new beginnings. Life is an endless cycle of endings and beginnings. Renewal and rebirth cannot occur without endings - as the new year's crop can only be planted and flourish in the decay of last year.

We must be willing to get rid of the life we've planned, so as to have the life that is waiting for us. The old skin has to be shed before the new one can come.
 - Joseph Campbell

Good Endings precede Good Beginnings.

If it isn't working, release it. If life isn't following the course you wanted, release your expectations and choose to love the life you have.

Every day is a new beginning - a day for a new plan and new action. If today, in conscious awareness, you choose the same plan as yesterday, you are wise. If you choose a different plan, you are equally wise. Whatever you choose, choose with intention.

The darkest night is often the bridge to the brightest tomorrow

The crops were planted, tended, and harvested - now the ground lies fallow, awaiting the new planting. Did the year fail? I think not.

As the year has seasons, everything in life has its own cycles - its own rhythms. There will be a Winter, Spring, Summer, and Autumn every year. Every creature will be born, reproduce (or not), and die. A tortoise may live a century and a butterfly a few hours, but each has a cycle.

The unpredictable and irregular happenings of life's cycles are an inherent part of their nature. There are droughts and heat waves, injuries occur. The lion eats the zebra - one is nourished, one dies - neither failed.

Careers and relationships also have their cycles of birth, growth, and death - to be followed by rebirth and the renewal of the cycle.

The ending of a job or a relationship may appear as the darkest night, but it is merely the Winter season - the time of renewal and rebirth that precedes the new planting - the beginning of the next great cycle.

40 - Begin Today

Standing in the inspiring vision of my future, I boldly take every step - large and small - with courage and intent.

Having set a direction, begin - begin today. Take action - take action every day.

Twenty years from now you will be more disappointed by the things you didn't do than by the ones you did do. So throw off the bowlines. Sail away from the safe harbor. Catch the trade winds in your sails. Explore. Dream. Discover.
- Mark Twain

There is no better time to begin than today - each and every "today." When obstacles stop you, think of new ways to reach your goals. In the words of the Oriental proverb, *Fall seven times, stand up eight.*

Faith is taking the first step even when you don't see the whole staircase.
- Martin Luther King, Jr.

Begin today. Act on your vision. Do your best. If you take action, you may succeed or you may fail, but if you do nothing, the only possible outcome is failure.

You are never too old to set another goal or to dream a new dream.
- C. S. Lewis

Every day is a new day - a day for new beginnings, new dreams, new action - a day for challenge, adventure , and discovery. TODAY, what is your goal? What is your dream? What action are you taking to further your goals and dreams?

Another Sunrise, Another New Beginning

Yesterday is dead. Tomorrow is a dream. Today - each today - is where the action is - where all of life occurs. Today IS your life - your only life. Life today to the fullest.

Let every day be the first day of the rest of your life, but especially let today be a new beginning, a renewal, a rebirth.

What is your vision for your life? Put it into action starting today.

Start Today: Whatever you want in life, start today. Not tomorrow - today. Let it be a small beginning - a tiny beginning. Your happiness depends on starting today - every day.

Begin Today, and Again Tomorrow

41 - Put Your Dreams Into Action

Powerful Dreams Inspire Powerful Action.
When You Can Taste, Smell, and Touch Your Dream, You Can Enroll the World.

Life is either a daring adventure or nothing.
Security is mostly a superstition. It does not exist in nature.
- Helen Keller

Every day is a day to take action. Whatever your choices, take action on those choices. Taking no action is equally a choice, just not a choice made from awareness. Make conscious choices, and take action on those choices - Today.

Today is your day to Spread Wing and Soar.
Fly Life on Free Wings, and Sing to its Glory.

Like a bird in flight, your life can soar above the troubles of the world. Breathe deep, choose, and break the shackles of your past. Don't wait. Do it today - and again tomorrow.

Act with Bold Courage - Standing in the inspiring vision of my future, I boldly take every step - large and small - with courage and intent.

Today is your day. What are you going to do today that you will thank yourself for tomorrow?

Fly Life on Free Wings, and Sing to its Glory
- Jonathan Lockwood Huie

42 - Gather Strength From Life's Storms

Today is your day to honor your being
Release each and every struggle.
Gather strength from life's storms.
Relax into the arms of spirit.

Today is a day to accept that life is often a struggle, and we sometimes end up bruised, battered and beaten. Accept the defeat and gather strength from it. Tomorrow, you will be stronger and better trained. Tonight, relax into the arms of Spirit, and sleep the childlike sleep of the noble warrior.

Life is not about waiting for the storm to pass - it's about learning to Dance in the Rain.
 - Vivian Greene

Gather strength from the storm

Honor your being,
Release each and
every struggle,
Gather strength
from life's storms,
Relax into the
arms of spirit.

- Jonathan Lockwood Huie

Is today a day to gather strength from the storm - a day to learn life lessons for the next battle? Or is today a day to sit by the fire and watch the storm rage outside? Either way, the storm is just life. Give thanks for all of Life.

Welcome the conquering Hero - and recognize that the Hero is... ourself.

The greatest battle of all is simply... Life. This is no child's game. This is the big one - the Super Bowl - the Game of all games. The rules of Life are unwritten and unknown. Perhaps, one could say that there are no rules. The Judge has ultimate power - She can call the game at any time - for any reason. The penalties in the Game are completely arbitrary - in both timing and severity. Penalty for what, we ask? The Judge is silent. How can I win the Game? "You can never win," comes the answer, "so just take pleasure in playing the Game."

43 - Love Your Job, or Get a New Career

If a man is called to be a street sweeper, he should sweep streets even as Michelangelo painted, or Beethoven composed music, or Shakespeare wrote poetry. He should sweep streets so well that all the hosts of heaven and earth will pause to say, here lived a great street sweeper who did his job well.
- Martin Luther King, Jr.

In the United States, my experience is that most people have an idea of what type of work makes a "good" job. Lawyer, doctor, and executive are good jobs. Writer, painter, and sculptor may be considered good jobs. Money and "prestige" make a job "good." Sweeping streets is NOT believed to be a good job, and those who take such jobs appear to consider them loathsome and shameful.

In contrast, I had a very different experience on my trip to New Zealand. People I met there actually were proud of their jobs - whatever they were. One man proudly told me that he was "the best bus boy in Christchurch." He was a very pleasant and well spoken man in his fifties who had been a clearing tables for 30 years. He was interested in Americans, and contrasted his happy life with the stories of stress he heard from the tourists whose tables he bussed.

Make a list of what you like and what you dislike about your job. Perhaps you enjoy your customers and co-workers, but find your boss annoying. Limit your awareness of the annoying times to the moment in which they occur, but let thoughts of the service and camaraderie permeate your day. If you find the frustrations of your job outweigh the enjoyment, get a new career. Whatever your interests, there is a way to do something you enjoy, make a difference in the world, and get well paid at the same time. Make a list of all your interests and abilities, and think big. Don't let anyone else's small and limited thinking deter you from your goal.

If a man is called to be a street sweeper, he should sweep streets even as Michelangelo painted, or Beethoven composed music, or Shakespeare wrote poetry. He should sweep streets so well that all the hosts of heaven and earth will pause to say, here lived a great street sweeper who did his job well.
- Martin Luther King, Jr.

44 - Have Gratitude for ALL of Life

I open to inspiration.
I open myself for the word of Spirit to flow through me.

When we accept all of Life with gratitude, we allow amazing and wonderful events to occur.

Be Grateful for All of Life: Each of us has been infinitely blessed - beginning with the gift of life. Whatever may appear to be missing or broken on any particular day, our glass is not half full, it is 99.9% full.

When we feel ungrateful, we become unhappy. When we choose to feel and express our gratitude, the act of feeling and speaking our thanks creates a happiness within us. The more we express our gratitude, the more we have for which to be grateful.

Today and every day, take time to celebrate life - whether an hour's meditation in a quiet natural space, or a brief moment's conscious pause to breathe deeply and celebrate gratitude for life.

Joy is what happens to us when we allow ourselves to recognize how good things really are.
- Marianne Williamson

Seeing your glass of life as mostly full triggers an amazing cycle of transformation. Appreciation for the abundance of life incites gratitude - which brings on that warm comfortable feeling of joy and satisfaction with life. Gratitude for abundance also creates increasing abundance. Being truly grateful for the abundance that is now in my life causes an ever greater abundance to flow in my direction.

Accept all of Life with gratitude.

45 - Be Open to Receiving Unlimited Abundance

Ask and it will be given to you; seek and you will find; knock and the door will be opened to you.
- Matthew 7:7

I Receive ALL of Life with Thanksgiving - I have gratitude for EVERYTHING that has ever occurred to bring me to this moment. I give thanks for the joys and the sufferings, the moments of peace and the flashes of anger, the compassion and the indifference, the roar of my courage and the cold sweat of my fear. I accept gratefully the entirety of my past and my present life.

I Receive ALL of Life with Thanksgiving - I have gratitude for EVERYTHING that has ever occurred to bring me to this moment. I give thanks for the joys and the sufferings, the moments of peace and the flashes of anger, the compassion and the indifference, the roar of my courage and the cold sweat of my fear. I accept gratefully the entirety of my past and my present life.
- Jonathan Lockwood Huie

46 - Make a Gratitude List, and Review It Often

Not everything has gone well in your life, but much has. Too often we focus on the negative and forget our great blessings - health, friends, family, beauty, nature, our body, our mind, Spirit, life itself. Perhaps you have arthritis or your spouse just moved out. Yes, those are big negatives, but your list, anyone's list, of blessings is vastly larger than any list of problems.

Start by finding things for which to be grateful. Gratitude is crucial to your happiness. If you are reading this article, you are alive and your brain is functioning fairly well. Start your gratitude list with living, breathing, and thinking. Add every blessing, however tiny, to your list. Every moment without pain is a blessing, every bite of food, every bird, tree, and butterfly. Give thanks for every "hello," and every smile.

Give thanks, also, for the life lessons. Make a list of what you have learned - yes, a written list. Be grateful for each lesson. Life lessons often come at great cost, but they are priceless jewels.

Have Gratitude For All Of Life: As with forgiveness, gratitude is a gift to yourself. Saying "thank you" is a powerful way to create great relationships, but the real power of gratitude is internalizing an immense thankfulness for your very existence - everything that has ever occurred or failed to occur in your life.

It's a beautiful world.

Take time today to appreciate beauty - natural beauty, art, people. Slow down, breathe deeply, smile. It's a beautiful world.

47 - Give Thanks for Your Thorns as well as Your Blooms

Today, I give thanks for both my bloom and my thorns.

We all have our thorns - and blooms. We, and Life, have our moments. Life occurs before our morning coffee. Life occurs in our bathrobe with our hair uncombed. Bless and give thanks for All of Life - the bloom and the thorns.

I give thanks for both my bloom and my thorns.
- Jonathan Lockwood Huie

48 - Learn to Relax in the Eye-of-the-Storm

There is beauty and serenity in the eye of the storm.

The Eye-of-the-Storm. Surrounded by the winds and the rain, yet peaceful in its own unworldly way - an unnatural ruddy-cloudy misty-bright kind of way. Whatever comes next, the eye of the storm is a moment of serenity among the challenge - a time for repose and contemplation.

Life is always lived in the eye-of-the-storm

Whatever the challenges that actually confront any of us on a given day, the potential threats are always far greater. There are always an array of catastrophes overhanging our lives - wars, terrorists, hurricanes, earthquakes, escaped murderers, child molesters, and maybe a runaway asteroid. In comparison with what "could" happen, our lives are rather serene.

Rather than worrying about the continuous stream of potential threats, let us give thanks for our blessing of living in the eye-of-the-storm - our protected refuge from the terrors of fearsome dangers just outside our lives.

Life is always lived in the eye-of-the-storm
- Jonathan Lockwood Huie

49 - Let Every Day be a Thanksgiving

Let Today be a Thanksgiving.

Every day, we have so much for which to be grateful. Let every day be a Thanksgiving. Let every day be a day we acknowledge our food, our family, our friends, our homes, our health, our very lives.

Food is a perfect symbol for all our gratitudes. Lift up a bowl of food in your fingertips, close your eyes, breathe deeply, and give thanks for Everything.

50 - Accept the Great Paradox of Life

A good traveler has no fixed plans, and is not intent on arriving.
- Lao Tzu

A great paradox of life is that while we must create plans for our future in order to live a joyful life, simultaneously, we must graciously accept whatever events life actually throws against us.

If we fail to plan, we merely bob helplessly - like a cork on the sea of life.
If we resist whatever life delivers to us, we create untold misery for ourselves.

Only by charting our course, and then continuously recharting that course in response to the events of life, can we achieve success and happiness.

We climb the steps to nowhere - always.

However carefully we plan our future, we are always climbing the steps to nowhere. While it is important to our happiness that we have an intent for our lives, it is equally crucial to accept in advance that we truly have no idea how our lives will turn out - and that is okay.

Our opportunity is to love ourselves exactly as we are - with all our joys and sufferings. To be grateful for everything. To forgive ourselves for our doubts of our own worthiness - for we have no need to be anything other than what we are.

Choose the World You See, and See the World You Choose.

Our opportunity is always to make the choice for Joy. To see the world with new eyes - open eyes - loving eyes. To choose compassion and understanding - for ourselves, our family, our friends, our community, for the whole world.

Our opportunity is to Soar our Spirit. To see Light and Joy in everything. To spread our wings and fly boldly. To give thanks for rainbows and butterflies - our symbols of renewal and rebirth. To offer daily Thanksgiving - for ourselves, our family, our friends, our community, for the whole world.

Our opportunity is to visualize a kinder world. To sing glad songs of tomorrow - imagining a world of love - of the whole world filled with love. To offer our hand... often. To breathe deeply and honor ourselves. To pause and contemplate... just because.

ɔ1 - Flow With the River of Life

The River of Life has no meaning - no good, no bad, no better, no worse, no love, no hate, no fear, no anger, no joy. The River of Life has no judgment, no expectation.
The River of Life just IS.

The River of Life meanders without apparent purpose. To question Life is to invite suffering. To attempt to overpower Life is to tilt at windmills. Life is best enjoyed without resistance.

Surrender to the flow of the River of Life, yet do not float down the river like a leaf or a log. While neither attempting to resist life nor to hurry it, become the rudder and use your energy to correct your course to avoid the whirlpools and undertow.

The River of Life
by Jonathan Lockwood Huie

The River of Life flows without emotion.
The River surges. The River quiets.
The River overflows its banks. The River dries to a trickle.
The River swirls and storms. The River becomes calm.
The River runs clear. The River runs dark with silt.
The River is indifferent to what benefit or what harm is caused by its water.
The River is the River, and that is all there is to it.

The River of Life has no judgments.
The River flows with no concept of good and bad - right and wrong.
The fields and dreams of men may be nourished by the River of Life, or flooded and covered with silt, and the River just flows.
Men may catch fish and live on the River of Life, or they may founder in a storm and drown, and the River just flows.

The River of Life is timeless.
It is not unchanging, but it is timeless, and it changes in its own time.

The River of Life knows no obstacles.
The River can cut through solid rock - in its own time.

The River of Life is not powerful - and it is not weak.
The River of Life is not gentle - and it is not strong or rough.
The River of Life is not deep or shallow.
The River of Life is not nourishing or punishing.
The River of Life is simply the River of Life.
The River of Life just IS. There is no more to it.

The River of Life has no meaning, no good, no bad, no better, no worse, no love, no hate, no fear, no anger, no joy.
The River of Life has no judgment, no expectation.
The River of Life just IS.

There is nothing to do.
There is nothing to say.
There is nothing to think.
There is nothing to feel.
The River just flows.

The River is the source of all nourishment - the source of all obstacles.
The River is the source of all life - the source of all death.
The River is the source of all joy - and the source of all sorrow.
Yet the River has no joy - and the River has no sorrow.
The River is just the River.

One can flow harmoniously with the River - or one can struggle fearfully against the River - and the River just flows.
One can accept the River - or one can deny the River - and the River just flows.
One can worship the River of Life - or one can curse the River of Life - and the River just flows.

There is nothing to do - and the River flows.
There is nothing to say - and the River flows.
There is nothing to think - and the River flows.
There is nothing to feel - and the River flows.
The River flows - and all else is our drama.
The River flows - and all else is our invention.

Choose to flow with the Rive of Life.

The River of Life has no meaning, no good, no bad, no better, no worse, no love, no hate, no fear, no anger, no joy. The River of Life has no judgment, no expectation. The River of Life just IS.   - Jonathan Lockwood Huie

52 - Don't Let Your Money and Possessions Own You

Often the simplest life is the happiest life.
Peace, Love, Health, Comfort, Joy, and the Light of Spirit - all the rest is nothing.

Most people think they own a home, furniture, computers, clothes, a bank account, and perhaps stocks. But perhaps they are owned by their possessions instead. Take the following quiz to see whether you are gaining happiness from your belongings, or whether you could find more happiness in a simpler lifestyle.

1. Write down the number of hours each week that you are conscious of enjoying your home. Subtract the number of hours you spend maintaining your home. Subtract the number of hours you work to have others maintain your home, to pay taxes, and to pay the mortgage. Now, subtract the number of hours you are conscious of worrying about paying for your home or about maintaining it.

2. Do you own a golf club membership, vacation home, boat, RV, sports or luxury car? Make the same computation as for your home - hours of enjoyment versus hours of work or worry.

3. Consider vacations, restaurant meals, expensive clothes and beauty treatments. Again compare hours of enjoyment to hours you spend working to pay for the luxury or worrying about its cost.

4. Do you live in fear of losing your job? Write down the worst things that would happen if you lost your job or source of income tomorrow.

Anything that costs you more hours of effort or worry than it brings you hours of enjoyment is a candidate for downsizing. The average American house size has more than doubled in the last 50 years. Has the average enjoyment of that home also doubled? How about the average worry?

Living in fear of anything is a terrible waste of what could be a great life. If you live in fear of losing your job, either you fear the embarrassment of being jobless, or you fear the loss of material goods - house, car, and such. If you live in fear of losing your stuff and money, they own you.

If you discover that your money and stuff do own you, you can regain your happiness either by downsizing, or by mentally accepting that downsizing would not be a terrible thing. Just the acceptance that a simpler lifestyle could be joyful is enough.

The only meaningful value in life is happiness, and happiness is dependent neither upon owning things nor upon renouncing material wealth, but rather upon consciously adopting an acceptance of whatever circumstances life throws your way.

53 - Enjoy Everything You Do, or Don't Do It

Yes, you have to file your taxes and stop at stop signs whether you like it or not. This secret refers to those things you do merely out of habit or to avoid embarrassment. Enjoy that party, or don't accept the invitation. Feel fulfilled by that volunteer committee, or don't join. Believe in that particular charitable cause, or don't contribute. Everything in life is a choice - make wise choices that maximize your happiness.

Exercise: Get comfortable and contemplate the following questions: How much time and energy do you spend on what you wear, and how much enjoyment do you get in return? What if clothes were merely something to keep you warm? Which aspects of personal grooming give you Joy, and which are burdens that you endure out of a fearful need for approval? How much time and energy do you spend on how you look, whether you are liked and respected, what you eat, your health, your bank account, your job, your retirement, your family, your safety, the weather, prices, shortages, government, big business, terrorists, crime, epidemics, foreign affairs, the economy, and everything on the 11 o'clock news? Do you get ample return in the form of enjoyment?

Our Joy comes from living our own lives simply - never from demanding that others live simply - or from ever making any demands whatsoever upon others.

Our Joy comes from living our own lives simply - never from demanding that others live simply - or from ever making any demands whatsoever upon others.
- *Jonathan Lockwood Huie*

54 - Simplify

He who is contented is rich.
- Lao Tzu

There is nothing I ever need to have.
There is nothing I ever need to do.
I say NO to the demands of the world.
I say YES to the longings of my own heart.

One of the secrets to a joyful life is Simplicity - saying NO to the advertisements for the latest this and the most glamorous that - saying NO to chasing that next job promotion - saying NO to all the stressful demands upon your time and energy.

There is nothing that you really NEED to have or NEED TO DO. Material possessions seldom bring joy. Consider eliminating whatever you haven't used in a year, and minimizing new purchases - not based on economy, but on your choice for leading a simple unencumbered life.

1. Simplify your needs: Much of our stress is due to what we believe we need to have. Actually, we need very little - food, a roof over our head, companionship. The rest is all perceived need that causes stress. As a crazy, but everyday example, we get stressed that we don't have the money to finance a relaxing vacation trip. Suppose we just relaxed every day knowing that we don't need luxuries.

2. Simplify your obligations: Practice saying "NO." No, I won't babysit your parakeet. No, I won't work a double shift Sunday. No, I won't chair the fundraising drive. There is actually almost nothing that you must do. Everything in life is a choice. Break the habit of assuming that you need to do everything you are asked to do.

He who is contented is rich
- Lao Tzu

55 - Adopt a Gentle and Supportive Lifestyle

Whatever you do, do with kindness.
Whatever you say, say with kindness.
Wherever you go, radiate kindness.

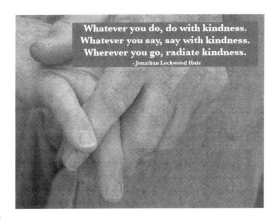

Care for your body and spirit with special attention and gentleness in this time of great challenge. Several times each day, take a moment to breathe deeply and center yourself. Consider beginning yoga or qigong. Eat healthy, keep hydrated. Get enough sleep. If you have trouble sleeping, pay special attention to the rest of the ideas in this secret, they will all help you sleep better.

Choose Inner Peace.

Nothing is worth losing your inner peace. Take action as circumstances require, but never surrender your inner peace. Stop. Breathe deeply. Close your eyes and breathe deeply again. Then, and only then, take action - from a peaceful heart.

I choose to flow with the River of Life.

Choose serenity by making a conscious choice to live a stress-free life. Stress is always waiting just outside your door like a vicious wild-dog, but a double-barreled defense can keep stress at bay.

The first weapon is choosing to see the lesson and the joy in each occurrence in your life.

The second is taking the time to find your moments of serenity and calm. Yes, that means making the choice of not doing something else, but do it anyway. Choose serenity.

I am Counterpoint to the Clamor of the World.

The world has always been in an uproar, and it always will be. Choose Peace. Choose to live with Peace. Choose to interact peacefully with everyone - especially those whose instinct is not to be peaceful.

56 - Give and Receive Love and Compassion

If you want others to be happy, practice compassion. If you want to be happy, practice compassion.
- Tenzin Gyatso, the 14th Dalai Lama

Consider the following parable. Perhaps no more need be said.

Where There is Love, Nothing is Missing - a Parable

The businessman looked around the vacation villa in Puerto Vallarta. Plain, but clean and well furnished. A good place to grab a few days away from his failing business and troubled marriage. He had brought a large supply of sleeping pills and had requested several bottles of Tequila to be brought to his room. Perhaps he could at least drown a few of his worries.

He watched as the housekeeper stocked the villa's kitchen - frozen dinners, some dry cereal, and thankfully, four large bottles of liquor - they had paid careful attention to his unusual requests. The frozen dinners would be easy - he could focus on his lonely drinking, and lose himself.

Jim noticed the housekeeper's slow movements, the stoop in her shoulders, the stubby yellowed teeth. It was somehow comforting to see that other people could be even worse off than he was. Even with his company troubles and impending divorce, Jim was sure he could always find the money to keep his teeth whitened and in good repair - even find the money for the hair transplant he had promised himself. He shivered a little, just thinking about those teeth.

The woman shuffled over to him. "Senor, you not look happy. TV dinner not good. I am Maria, I cook. I bring you real food."

"OK, OK." Jim didn't want to talk with anyone, and certainly not with this woman. Besides, a taco might be better than microwave food - if it showed up on his table.

The bustling in the kitchen brought Jim out of the depths of his hangover. It hadn't been a really big night - less than a whole bottle of booze, and none of the sleeping pills - he might want to take those all at once. Still, he felt really lousy, and resented the intrusion. The bedside clock showed 12:30 as Maria opened the curtains and sunlight poured in.

The enticing smells of spicy meat and corn filled the villa. Maria stood over him, offering a plate of tamales. "Senor, eat. You feel better."

Jim reached for one, took a hesitant bite, and relaxed a little. Before he knew it, the heaping plate was almost empty.

Maria moved the nearly empty plate to the kitchen counter. "You were hungry. Get a nice hot bath. I come back," and she moved toward the door.

"How much do I owe you," Jim called out, remembering her apparent poverty.

"Nothing. My gift. You were hungry," and she was gone.

The next afternoon, Chiles Rellenos appeared. Jim had drunk less the second night, and was even more appreciative of the good food. Again, Maria would not accept payment. "I have money. You must need money, please take it," Jim almost pleaded. Maria replied, "I am rich. Please come to my home tonight. I will show you. I come back at seven."

At exactly 7 PM, there was a knock on the door. Jim followed Maria into the warm twilight. They walked silently through the tourist area, then turned sharply down an alley. They emerged into a neighborhood of partially finished stucco dwellings. Iron reinforcing rods spiked the tops of the unfinished verticals. Plastic sheeting substituted for glass in the unfinished windows. Maria led Jim to one of the unfinished stairways and began to climb.

Opening a door on the fourth floor, Maria smiled at Jim and beckoned him to enter. The walls and floor were bare except for small rugs and weavings that combined bright reds, oranges, and yellows. A small sofa and a few chairs lined the walls, one of which honored an oversized Madonna-with-child picture featuring a dark-skinned Mary. The small room was dominated by a long plank table covered with food and surrounded by a dozen happy-looking eaters of all shapes and ages - newborns to nineties. The delicious smells welcomed Jim.

Near tears, Jim turned to Maria to thank her, but words didn't form.

Leading Jim to the table, Maria introduced him to her family, saying, "I am rich. I have my family. Where there is love, nothing is missing. My family is now your family."

Where There is Love, Nothing is Missing

- *Jonathan Lockwood Huie*

57 - Look for the Best in People

Life is a reflection of intent.
Love reflects love.
Hate reflects hate.

Everyone has good points and bad. Everyone will please you at times and annoy you at others. While there is power in choosing to associate mostly with positive people, there is even more power in seeing the best in everyone. Everyone has a lesson to teach us. Let the impact of an unkind or thoughtless word last only a moment, but bask for a whole day in gentle words and insightful thoughts.

The happiest among us have no enemies.

58 - Build an Emotional Support System

Do you have a support system - friends and family you can confide in? If so, be very grateful, and use that network now. Don't be embarrassed to seek emotional support from those you respect and love. If you don't feel you have a support network, find one in your church or community, and be grateful for those who are willing to be of service.

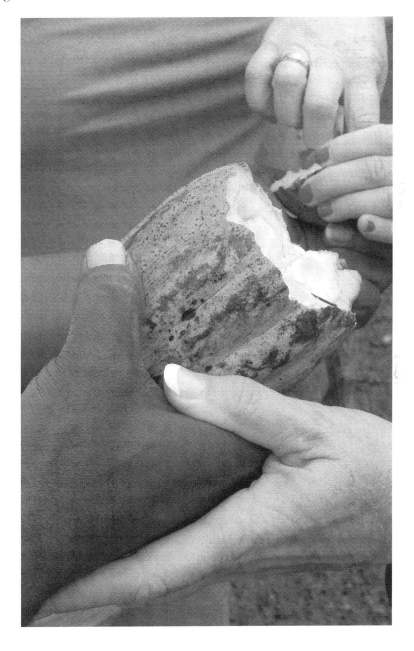

59 - Associate Mostly With Positive People

It is far better to be alone, than to be in bad company.
 - George Washington

Of course you can and should keep your composure and happiness regardless of circumstances - regardless of your friends, family and co-workers - regardless of gossip, sarcasm, and negativity. Nonetheless, life is much easier and more pleasant when you spend as much time as possible in the company of enthusiastic positive people - not necessarily those who agree with you, but those who respect your right to your point of view.

Happiness: It Really Is Contagious

You have probably noticed that where you find one happy person, you are likely to find a whole group of happy people. Perhaps you have a guess at why that is so. Happy people seek out other happy people? I'm sure that is a major factor, but the other explanation - that happiness is contagious - has recently been verified by University researchers.

It is far better to be alone
than to be in bad company
- George Washington

60 - Appreciate Your Friends

It's the friends you can call up at 4 a.m. that matter.
- Marlene Dietrich

When you can call them at 4 AM they have become family - real family - perhaps even more real family than your blood relatives. Honor them, and give thanks for them.

My Chosen Family
You are my family, but we don't share blood.
You are my family by choice.
The most powerful bond is the one that we choose.
I choose you as my friend, and rejoice.

Some of us have relationships with our blood relatives that are uncertain at best, but that doesn't mean that we can't enjoy a loving family. The most wonderful family is the one we Choose - whether we happen to share blood with them or not. Have deep gratitude for your Chosen family.

It's the friends you can call up at 4 a.m. that matter. - Marlene Dietrich

61 - Appreciate Your Family

Honor thy family.

Our loved ones - whether by blood, by marriage, or by choice - are delicate treasures. If we hold them too close, they break - as a butterfly would. By honoring and enjoying the freedom of our loved ones, we gain our own freedom. Have the courage to trust that the beautiful butterflies of your life will return - or not - as life intends.

I choose to enjoy people as I enjoy a rainbow or a butterfly - they are most beautiful when they are free.

Today is a day to remember our family with honor. Whatever our relationship with our blood family, and however close we have become to those who have become our family of choice, today is a day to honor our heritage.

62 - Appreciate Your Life Partner

Home is where our loved ones are.

A palace is not a home without loved ones. A shack or an open field can be paradise when shared with a loving family.

I love you not only for what you are, but for what I am when I am with you.
I love you not only for what you have made of yourself, but for what you are making of me.
I love you for that part of me you bring out.
- Elizabeth Barrett Browning

My Loved One
You are my ground and you are my rainbow.
You are my butterfly and you are my ecstasy.
You are the start of my journeys and always my destination.
You are my home - the place to which I always return.

63 - Express Your Honest Appreciation

Give Honest and Sincere Appreciation
- Dale Carnegie

When I was very young, my mother gave me gold stars whenever I did something she liked. Usually they were small gold foil shapes with sticky backs, but Mother also saved some really big ones - three inches across - for extra-special accomplishments. Together with Mother's love, those stars made me feel special, important, and appreciated.

As adults, we are much more likely to receive criticism than appreciation. Our boss, our spouse, and the others in our lives expect much from us. When we fail to live up to their expectations, they criticize, but when we go beyond the call, or better yet do something delightfully unexpected, we are likely to get an "ummm..." response at best.

Appreciation, whether verbal or as physical shiny gold stars, is perhaps the greatest gift we can give to those around us. In the timeless *How to Win Friends and Influence People*, Dale Carnegie lists "Give Honest and Sincere Appreciation," as one of his fundamental principles.

When was the last time you offered sincere appreciation or a gold star? Perhaps it was recently. In a few offices, gold stars have become a common, if sometimes insincere, practice. Some on-line communities provide gold stars - or green stars or butterflies - for members to award each other. However, most of the time most of us fail to express our appreciation to those people who make our lives better in small, or large, ways.

Consider these ways to express appreciation:

1. Give someone a shiny gold star. It's only tacky or childish if your action is insincere.

2. Send a note of appreciation. Again, if it's sincere, it's always gracious and never inappropriate.

3. Speak your appreciation directly. Say "I appreciate what you did."

4. Say "Thank You" as often as you can.

5. Express appreciation for the person as well as the deed. "I appreciate YOU. Thank You for being my friend - or co-worker, or..."

Give somebody a gold star - Today.

64 - Be of Service

Lord, grant that I might not so much seek to be loved as to love.
- St. Francis of Assisi

Is someone you know going through a difficult time? You want to be helpful, but how? It is possible that you can help with money or material things. It is possible that you can use your time to perform services for them. It is also possible, although unlikely, that your well-intentioned advice will serve them well.

Generally, your greatest service to someone in their time of trouble, sorrow, or confusion, is your comfort. Take the time to listen to their troubles and concerns with patience, kindness, and empathy, but without offering unsolicited advice or suggestions. Your kindly hand on their shoulder, supportive hug, and patient listening are often the greatest gifts you can offer.

Service becomes a source of joy when it is not viewed as a duty.

Lord, grant that I might not so much seek to be loved as to love
- St. Francis of Assisi

65 - Stay in Your Own Business

Caring about someone is not an excuse to try to live their life for them - that's meddling. If you choose to be helpful, help others to achieve the life THEY desire, rather than the life you wish for them.

Many of us get upset - and stressed - over the actions of others that are really none of our business. The lifestyle of others is NOT our business. Whether your adult son or daughter has a job, whether they married the "wrong" partner, whether your neighbor recycles, whether the man down the street watches adult movies or his wife is having an affair - these are NOT our business.

Know that there is no single way that life is "supposed" to be. Demanding that life meet our expectations is a sure fire recipe for a miserable existence. Life is a game with no rules. Have NO Expectations of life. Stay in your own business and lower your stress.

Minding other people's business doesn't create happiness for them or for me. In the words of the old saying, "Live and let live." Between living my own life and my commitment to sow a few seeds of joy in the world, my life is quite full, thank you.

Nonetheless, I continue to find myself meddling in the affairs of others. All too often my intention to be supportive and generous runs amok. In the aftermath, I tell myself that I will never do that again, but I do. In a way, I wouldn't want it otherwise. The line between "helpful" and meddling is so easy to cross. The only way that I could ensure that I never meddled would be to completely disavow being helpful.

Byron Katie speaks of *my business, your business, and God's business.* Everything that happens in the world, or doesn't happen, is NOT my responsibility. There are more than enough things that are my responsibility. I am responsible for my thoughts, my beliefs, and my actions - and that is enough. It does not serve me to mind anyone else's business. I can only make myself unhappy by trying to second guess what anyone else thinks or does.

That's all easy enough to say in the abstract, but when the other person is our friend, spouse, parent, adult son or daughter, or co-worker, it doesn't come at all naturally to remain detached. For many of us, staying in our own business requires a lifetime of self-reminders.

Often we meddle out of a sincere desire to help another, so how can we know when we have gone too far? We have overstepped our bounds whenever we cross the line from assisting others in getting what they want to believing that we know better than they what they SHOULD want.

Through painful experience, I have found five questions to ask myself to help determine whether I am providing assistance or meddling.

1. Did the other person ask for help, advice, or opinion? If the answer is No, then I am meddling. The first and greatest rule is,

Unsolicited Advice Is Always Meddling

2. Even if the person has broadcast a request for help or advice, did they ask for MY advice? When someone is drowning, they will accept a life-ring thrown by a stranger, but advice is only appreciated if the asker fully trusts and respects the advisor.

3. Do I fully respect the other person? While I can responsibly make decisions for a child or a senile person, it is pure meddling for me to believe that I know better than another competent adult how they should live their life. As an example, trying to find friends for someone who has clearly expressed a preference for solitude is meddling.

4. Is the issue a question of belief? Proselytizing is always meddling. My beliefs about religion, politics, the best natural supplements, or whatever, are just my personal beliefs, nothing more. If someone ASKS, I am happy to share about what gives my own life joy and meaning, but whenever I attempt to convert someone else's beliefs, I must be very clear that I am doing it for my own gains, and not as a service to the other.

5. Have I previously attempted to assist this person with this same issue in the past? If I have been asked again, and if I find a different way to be helpful, it's not meddling, but if I continually offer the same advice for the same problem, it crosses the line into meddling.

Compassion and generosity may well be the greatest human virtues, but it is also important to avoid letting these noble instincts cause inadvertent harm to those we want to help.

Unsolicited Advice Is Always Meddling

- Jonathan Lockwood Huie

66 - Receive Graciously and Gratefully

A great gift requires two people, the giver and the receiver. Think of a football pass… Skillfully catching the pass, the gift, is fully as important, and difficult, as throwing it.

In many ways, it is easier to be a good giver than a good receiver. The giver chooses the gift and the timing. More important, societal and religious traditions tend to elevate the status of giver, and lower the status of receiver.

A wonderful gift may not be wrapped as you expect.
- Jonathan Lockwood Huie

I received an email asking, "I know exactly the kind of man I want. Why am I not finding him?" My answer was, "Perhaps by being so sure that you know what you want in a man you are overlooking some great possible partners. A wonderful gift may not be wrapped as you expect."

The principle of intent is not just applicable to dating, but is universal. Intention is a powerful force, but contains a hidden paradox.

If you have no idea what you want from life, you have no power to call anything important and satisfying into being. Therefore, envision your desire as a full color dream with surround sound. Make your dream very detailed, and so real you can smell and taste it.

However, Spirit has its own idea of what great gifts to give you. Once you have made your request, be open to receiving the bounty of the universe. Most likely, your gift will not look exactly as you visualized it. Be open to every phone call, every knock at the door.

The secret to accessing the power of intention is to follow two seemingly contradictory paths at the same time:

1. Visualize what you want. Plan and take positive action to achieve your goal.

2. Always be open to receiving the generous gifts of Spirit. Hold no expectations or demands on the form, the timing, or the color of the wrapping on the bountiful gifts of Spirit.

Affirmation: *I am open to receiving the bountiful gifts of Spirit. My mind and heart are open.*

67 - Make Peace with Your Past through Forgiveness

In the words of William Shakespeare, "What's done is done." You can't change the past. You can't undo any actions you took or failed to take. Your only choice today is either to waste energy and emotion on regrets and resentments, or to treat your own past like a history book - an interesting, but emotionally neutral, recitation of ancient times.

The ugliest word in the world is revenge.
It spells hate; it spells fear; it spells greed.
For my loss, I must kill; I must steal - must avenge.
It's your fault; you must pay; you must bleed.

Give yourself the gift of forgiving everyone you are angry with - for every action you resent.

Forgive Everyone for Everything. Angry and happy don't mix. Flush out the angry, and the happy has a place to put down roots. Until we forgive everyone for everything, we hold on to anger and resentment. Once we forgive, we can become happy. Forgiving is not a gift to someone else. Forgiving is our gift to ourselves - a great gift - the gift of happiness.

Forgiveness is a gift to yourself. YOU created the stress in your life by getting angry, and YOU can instantly remove that stress by granting forgiveness. Expressing your forgiveness to the other is optional - internalizing that forgiveness is required in order to live a joyful life. Don't forget to also forgive yourself for everything you regret ever having done or not done.

Affirmation: *I Forgive Myself and All Others with Compassion. I forgive everyone, especially myself, for all actions and all inactions throughout my entire life. I accept that no one else has ever been to blame for either my joy or my suffering. The entire cause of all my joys and all my sufferings is my own emotional response to the events of my life, and I am committed to consistently distinguishing between my feelings about events and the physical occurrence of those events. I declare that everyone who has ever played any role in any of the events of my life is entirely without fault.*

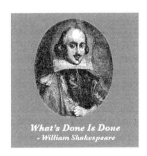

What's Done Is Done
- William Shakespeare

68 - Forgive Everyone For Everything

"I can forgive, but I cannot forget," is only another way of saying, I will not forgive. Forgiveness ought to be like a canceled note - torn in two, and burned up, so that it never can be shown against one.
- Henry Ward Beecher

Wise words from Henry Ward Beecher, 19th century Congregationalist clergyman and social reformer, but still... How to cancel, tear up, and burn the burden of resentment that darkens our hearts and burdens our spirit?

Complete forgiveness of everyone, including yourself, for all actions and inactions is the key to happiness, but... How to do it? It is one thing to pass the hurdle of agreeing in concept that forgiving would relieve your own tremendous burden of resentments, regrets, anger, and hatred, but it is quite another thing to accomplish that forgiving.

This is how I strive to move past my resentments so I can gain peace and no longer be haunted by anger and hate...

1. I recognize that the person who harmed me was a troubled person who probably did not intend to do me personal harm. I just happened to be at the wrong place at the wrong time.

2. I consciously remind myself whenever resentments reoccur that my anger burns me rather than him.

3. I remind myself that the events are now in the past with, in some sense, no more reality than last night's bad dream.

4. I am grateful for the lessons I have learned. Yes, I have learned to be more suspicious of people, but much more important, I have learned crucial life lessons about my own attitudes and responses.

5. I have so much else for which to be grateful. I am very grateful for my family, my home, good food, my health, and so much more. I am one of the most fortunate humans on this planet, and simply being granted humanity at all is the most amazing gift.

69 - Purge the Ghosts of Your Childhood (more forgiveness)

Forgiveness is the cleansing fire that burns away old regrets and resentments.

Forgiving is not a gift to someone else. Forgiving is your gift to yourself - a great gift - the gift of happiness.

But what if something REALLY terrible was done to you, for example a childhood sexual molestation? The irony is that the more terrible the event, the more peace you can gain by forgiving it.

Forgiving and accepting does NOT mean that what was done was okay. An injustice was done, and someone likely should be punished. But your anger and resentment don't punish the other person. Your anger and resentment only punish you. So stop it. Stop it now. Stop hurting yourself and issue your own proclamation of forgiveness and acceptance so YOU can finally stop suffering.

The key to achieving the freedom of forgiveness is reinterpreting your resentments so they no longer haunt you.

1. Attempt to see the event from the other person's point of view. By this, I do not mean how you believe they should have perceived the event, or how you believe that you would have perceived the event standing in their shoes, but how you can imagine, with generosity, that they actually perceived the event at the time it occurred.

2. Although we know logically that the event happened in the past, we tend to feel as if we are being injured in the present moment. Concentrate on viewing the event as history, rather than as something that is occurring now.

3. See the event as a great, if expensive, lesson. Make a list of all you have learned from the event. Focus on the positive lessons rather than the lesson of not trusting people. Let the lessons include having more gratitude for everything you are blessed with each day.

70 - Learn the #1 Secret of Great Relationships

The number one secret of great relationships is,
I Love You Just the Way You Are

Happiness lies in accepting everyone in our lives EXACTLY as they are. We cause ourselves untold misery whenever we believe others to be imperfect and try to change them. This is the number one rule for a happy relationship.

What could be a more appreciated sentiment than, "I love you just the way you are." No pretense. No hoping for change. No thought that it used to be better or might get better.

The greatest cause of relationship conflict is, "I wish you were different" or "Please change." Wishing or hoping your loved one would change is no way to show your love. Trying to force them to change through bribes or threats is even worse.

Celebrate your relationship by telling your loved one, "I love you just the way you are." Really mean it, and follow through by living into that sentiment each day for the rest of your lives.

I love you just the way you are

71 - Date Sensibly (for Women)

You are in love. Your hormones are surging, so you know this must be "the one." Besides, you are lonely and you want someone to hold you and make you feel cherished - now. "Mister Right" is saying all the things you want to hear. He says he adores you and wants you forever. STOP! Review this list of what it takes for a relationship to stay great over the years.

7 Keys to a Great Relationship

1. You are Self-Reliant. "Neediness" is no basis for a relationship. If you feel that you "need" him, or that you "need" to be in relationship, STOP! You are not ready for this or any other relationship. Do some personal work on yourself first. It isn't fair to him or to yourself to merge your lives before you love and respect yourself.

2. He is Self-Reliant. If he "needs" you, RUN. Choose someone who is already happy with himself and his life. While being "needed" may stroke your ego now, just fast forward a few months. Visualize him clinging to you and being jealous whenever you want a night with the girls. Moreover, if he is a person who is not satisfied with his life now, know that you are NOT the "magic pill" that will keep him happy over the years. Choose a happy and self-reliant man who views you as the magnificent frosting on the cake of his already wonderful life.

3. He Respects you and respects women in general. Disrespect is fatal to a relationship - both disrespect for you and disrespect in general. If he is EVER sarcastic or demeaning to you, end it now - even if it only happens once and he apologizes profusely. If he shows disrespect now while he is courting you, I guarantee it will get worse over time. A particular caution is to avoid men who have a general disrespect for women as a group. These are hopeless relationship candidates. You are NOT an exception; if your prospective partner disrespects those of your gender, he will NOT respect you - however fervently he promises that you are different. If he says something like, "Most women are bitches, but you are different; you are special," RUN, run fast, run far, never look back. Choose a man who demonstrates respect toward himself, toward you, and toward everyone else.

4. He is Gentle. Hopefully it is obvious that if he EVER raises a hand to you or threatens, leave instantly - and stop in at your local police station. Don't ask for an apology; don't say anything; just get away.

5. You are not "Rescuing" or Pitying him. If you are looking for a forlorn puppy, try your local animal shelter. If you are looking for a charitable cause, volunteer at the food bank. But, if you are looking for a life partner, make sure that his acting helpless is not part of his appeal to you. If he can't match his socks without your help, or hasn't cooked himself a healthy meal in weeks, or says he doesn't have any

friends, Run. Your job is to co-create a great life with your partner - not to "fix" him.

6. You like his Friends and Family. His friends and family are crucial to the success of your relationship. If you haven't met them yet, do it now - don't wait another minute. His friends and family are his life. Whatever he says, he won't give them up for you; it's not in his nature. If he is tied to his mother's apron strings, you want to know that today. If you dislike his friends now, you will hate them later. Choose a man who brings great friends and family to your relationship.

7. You accept him EXACTLY as he is and promise never to try to change him. He is practically perfect except he drinks too much, or smokes, or swears, or spends too much time with his friends, or does something else that really bugs you. Get REAL. He isn't going to change! He may promise to change in order to woo you. He may really feel committed to changing. But it isn't going to happen. Respect him, love him, and accept him EXACTLY as he is today, or break it off, and find someone you respect and accept exactly as they are today.

72 - Date Sensibly After Divorce (for Men)

You say you are looking for your next long term relationship - this time a really great lifelong partnership - but you are horny and you want to get laid - soon. STOP! That attitude is NOT going to lead you to a great long term relationship. Bank the fires of lust long enough to search consciously for a truly compatible match.

Before You Look For A Great Relationship…

1. Understand what went wrong the last time. Exactly the same things that went wrong last time WILL go wrong again, unless you analyze the issues and take specific steps to ensure that your next relationship is different.

You will be bringing the same "you" to your next relationship - unless you change. You will be attracted to the same kind of woman - unless you become more conscious in your choosing. You and your next partner will push each other's emotional "buttons" in the same ways - unless you examine your sensitivities.

Be TOTALLY honest with yourself about which of your needs were not met the last time, and which of your habits became intolerable to your previous wife.

2. Be sure you are ready. "Neediness" is no basis for a relationship. If you feel that you "need" a woman, or that you "need" to be in relationship, STOP! You are not ready to begin any relationship. Do some personal work on yourself first. It isn't fair to a partner or to yourself to merge your lives before you love and respect yourself.

3. Double-check your motives. If you are just looking for sex, don't pretend to yourself that you want relationship. Be sure that you are looking for a fully-engaged give-and-take partnership with a strong teammate.

4. Make a Shopping List. If this sounds a little impersonal, good. BEFORE you start meeting women, make your list, and have a strong talk with yourself about not compromising on ANY of the crucial items on your list. Make a list of perhaps five "must have's" and five "can't stand's." Make sure that you have included the really critical issue.

When you are ready to begin looking…

1. Look where the women are. Find a place where the ratio is strongly in your favor - a place with lots of available women who match your criteria for a long term partner.

2. Try on-line dating. You get to meet a lot of women quickly, and you learn some objective information before you meet in person. Consider the old story of the

mother who insisted that her daughter only date millionaires. Her explanation was "If you meet enough millionaires, you will certainly fall in love with one of them."

If you want someone to share your beliefs on religion, child rearing, sex and the other basics where differences greatly stress or fracture relationships, check out these issues before you even meet the woman. Don't let yourself get infatuated with someone who holds a fundamentally different outlook on life. Prevent the suffering by never even meeting.

3. Choose an on-line dating service that does the matching. Be completely honest in filling out your profile. Remember that your objective is to get a great lifelong match rather than a quick hot date. Be patient. CAUTION, people can lie anywhere, and a few do, so never take anything at face value.

You have met someone, now what?

1. Slow Down! No sex until you have checked her out. Once you get sex, you are hooked. Keep your options open until you are sure.

2. Look at the quality of her current life. If her life is a mess, Run. You don't need a one-sided relationship with someone who is "helpless" and needs you to "fix" her. If she "needs" you, RUN.

Look for a woman who is already happy with herself and her life. While being "needed" may stroke your ego now, just fast forward a few months. Visualize her clinging to you and being jealous whenever you want a night with the boys. Moreover, if she is a person who is not satisfied with her life now, know that you are NOT the "magic pill" that will keep her happy over the years.

Look for a happy and self-reliant woman who views you as the magnificent frosting on the cake of her already wonderful life.

3. Check out her friends and family. Her friends and family are crucial to the success of your relationship. If you haven't met them yet, do it now - don't wait another minute. Her friends and family are her life. If she is tied to her mother's apron strings, you want to know that today. If you dislike her friends now, you will hate them later. Choose a woman who brings great friends and family to your relationship.

4. Accept her EXACTLY as she is today and promise never to try to change her. If she is practically perfect except she talks too much, or smokes, or does something else that really bugs you, STOP. She isn't going to change! She may promise to change in order to reel you in. She may really feel committed to changing. But it isn't going to happen. Respect her, love her, and accept her EXACTLY as she is today, or break it off, and find someone you respect and accept exactly as they are.

73 - Be Yourself When You Are Dating

Guys are supposed to act confident, buy flowers, tell jokes. Gals are told to hang on his every word, flirt, be coy. Baloney! Why be a pretend you - an imitation you - instead of a real you? As Judy Garland said, "Always be a first-rate version of yourself, instead of a second-rate version of somebody else."

Why are you dating? If you are dating because you like to go on first dates, then fine - just play the actor or actress - and enjoy an evening of make believe. However, if you are dating because you want someone in your life longer term, stop the play-acting and be yourself.

The role-playing is completely counterproductive for two reasons. First, suppose that you are successful in impressing and attracting your date with your antics. What happens later when you let your guard down and revert to being yourself? You will be unmasked as not being the person your date was attracted to, and revealed as a phony beside.

The even more unfortunate situation occurs when your date is not attracted to your contrived persona, but would have loved the real you. What a huge loss to be on a date with the man or woman of your dreams and never even recognize them or have them recognize you because each of you was so busy play-acting.

What to do:

1. Clear the air. Before your first date, or on your first date at the latest, announce that you are going to relax and be yourself, and invite your date to be himself or herself as well. Some dates won't know what to make of that invitation, but the person you really want in your life will respond with gratitude, and will also relax.

If you are using an on-line dating service, be sure that your profile reflects the real you - without any puffery or distortion of your true qualities. Be proud of who you are, and share your true self. Have the "clear the air" conversation before you meet in person.

2. Choose relaxed places for your first few dates. There are environments that foster play-acting, and there are those that support each of you in being yourself. Choose the latter. For example, choose a picnic or a day at the zoo rather than a nightclub. Get to know your date without alcohol.

3. Ask for feedback. Dating is often a time for playing the guessing game as well as the play-acting game. Don't guess, ask how your date is feeling, what they want to do or not do. Give your date the same consideration as you would give a good friend.

4. Just remember to relax and be yourself. You will enjoy your date more - and you will create an opening for a wonderful long-term relationship with someone who likes the real you.

Always be a first-rate version of yourself, instead of a second-rate version of somebody else.
- Judy Garland

74 - Learn How to Make Your Relationship Great

Why do some couples stay happy together for a lifetime, while others are in conflict almost from the beginning?

Part of the answer is compatibility - making the initial choice of a partner with whom you share common values. Equally much, however, depends upon the choices each partner makes during the relationship. Here are seven choices made by happy couples...

1. Trust: Suspicion and jealousy are the death knell of any relationship. If the other is going to cheat or otherwise dishonor the relationship, suspicion and jealousy will not prevent it, and such a relationship is fatally flawed in any case. Unwarranted suspicion and jealousy create misery in a surprising number of relationships. If you want to live happily, trust your partner completely. If they dishonor your trust, deal with the situation then. In the meanwhile, you will have been happy.

2. Open Communication: Tell the truth, tell the whole truth. If you didn't want to share your whole life with your partner, why are you together? If you make a mistake, admit it. If you have doubts, talk about them. Secrets and lies kill a relationship. With truth and openness greatness is possible. Even if something is unforgivable, it is better to deal with it quickly.

3. Honoring the other's point-of-view: People disagree, couples disagree. Understanding that the two partners in a couple remain individuals is crucial to a happy relationship. Why would you expect that you and your partner should agree on everything? Honor that one of you is a Republican and the other a Democrat. Honor that one of you is a vegetarian and the other loves a great steak.

4. Self-Confidence: Co-dependence is another frequent cause of failed relationships. Happy couples know that they don't need each other. Each partner is a completely whole and valid individual who has entered into a voluntary partnership. Neither "owns" the other, nor "can't live without" the other. Each has their own interests and friends, as well as having mutual interests and friends.

5. Generosity: Greed and selfishness kill relationships. True love is generous in spirit. Mostly, generosity is not about material things, although that is also important. To have a happy relationship, be generous of your time, your love, and your attention.

6. Forgiveness: Resentments and thoughts of revenge and vengeance have no place in a happy relationship. Happy couples forgive each other completely for everything the other has ever done or failed to do - no exceptions.

7. Gratitude: Happy couples are continuously grateful for each other. Every day there are a myriad of reasons to be grateful for your partner. Find those reasons each day, and thank your partner every day.

75 - Avoid These Relationship Killers

Disrespecting and belittling one's partner will surely kill a relationship, and it will be an ugly and tortured death.

Sometimes disrespect is intentional, but sometimes it is unconscious, perhaps growing out of bad habits of speech or patterns of interaction. For example, joking about one's partner can cross the line over the years.

The following behaviors are all relationship killers…

1. Using the "Spousal We": "We need to remember to take out the garbage." "Didn't we make a fool of ourself at the party last night."

2. Using guilt: Be clear that "guilt" is a verb. It is a weapon that can devastate your partner. The partner using guilt makes sure that the other always knows how "wrong" they are, and how "unfair" their every action is. Their very existence is wrong and unfair.

3. Using sarcasm: Sarcasm is like a cluster bomb. "Well, I see we are still watching TV." Triple whammy relationship killer - guilt, sarcasm, and the spousal we.

4. Making an endless "honey do" list: This is usually combined with guilt by emphasizing how "fair" the list builder is being. The list builder is quick to pad everything they contribute to the relationship while minimizing the contributions of the other.

5. Acting jealous: Jealousy isn't teasing or flirting, it is irrational anger, which is often expressed randomly. Say you just came out of a restaurant, and you are driving home. "Weren't we just something in there. I saw how you looked at that waitress/waiter. I was SO embarrassed. You should be SO ashamed."

6. Having concealed expectations: If this sounds like concealed weapons, you got the idea, because expectations are dangerous weapons that kill relationships. "You should have known that I only like pink roses." "How could you not come home early on a day I'm feeling depressed?" "It's my birthday, and you get me socks?"

76 - Test the Soundness of Your Relationship

Do you have the occasional argument? Do you sometimes you feel frustrated, or have that uneasy sense that everything is not as it should be? Is your relationship in trouble? Ask yourself these questions to measure the overall state of your relationship and highlight the trouble spots.

1. When you have an argument, is it about a specific issue, or is it about your partner's character? A specific issue would be, "You forgot to take out the garbage last night," while "You never remember anything," is a generalized character assassination.

2. Do you have more conflict or less conflict when the two of you get time alone together? Do a "date night" or a few days away renew your relationship, or create more stress?

3. Is there physical violence in your relationship? Have you come close to physical violence? Are there threats of physical violence?

4. How often does the thought that you would rather be with someone else pass through your mind?

5. Take one minute to write a list of what you like and what you dislike about your partner. How many "likes" and how many "dislikes" are on your list?

6. Do you seriously question your partner's faithfulness?

7. Do you have arguments about sex?

8. In times of emergency or grief - such as when a relative becomes ill or dies, do you and your partner pull together?

9. If you could turn the clock back to the day you first met your partner, would you choose a different direction for your life?

10. If you won the lottery, would you be overjoyed to share the blessing with your partner, or would you wish it were all yours?

Physical violence or threats are the biggest danger signs for your relationship and for your personal safety. If they are present, get professional help TODAY.

The following are all danger signs for your relationship. If several are present, your relationship is in real trouble:

* character assassination

* fantasizing often about being with someone else
* not having ready access to a list of your partner's great qualities
* doubts of faithfulness
* serious sexual incompatibility
* lack of mutual support in times of crisis
* a feeling of being stuck or obligated by the relationship

Question #2 offers hope that your relationship may be much sounder than it appears. Conflict in your relationship may be primarily a reflection of the stress in your individual lives.

Often, partners redirect frustration and anger about unrelated events toward each other. For example, your boss yelled at you, and you yell at your partner. This unconscious redirection is a behavior that can be overcome through conscious attention, and is not a reflection on the overall quality of your relationship. If you and your partner are loving and supportive toward each other in relatively stress-free situations, you likely have a basis for working through your other issues.

77 - Find Happiness Beyond the Grief of Divorce

If you have been divorced, you know it hurts - especially if your marriage had lasted many years. Whatever the circumstances of your relationship, and whatever the nature of its ending, there is always grief and regret - perhaps regret over the ending or perhaps regret over not ending the relationship sooner - or perhaps both.

How to move past the grief and regret? No matter how painful, divorce, like all endings, opens the door to new beginnings. Let's examine several.

1. Get support: Don't be embarrassed to ask friends for support. Join a divorce support group. Join a more general women's or men's group and share your story.

2. Reconsider your obligations: In reality, you have NO obligations. There is nothing you ever have to do, because everything you do or don't do is always a choice. Be especially clear that you don't owe anyone an explanation or justification for any of your actions - ever.

3. Try something new: What have you been wanting to do, but couldn't find the time or commitment to begin? Perhaps yoga, qigong, stretching, walking, a new spiritual class, a book discussion group, ballroom dancing.

4. Learn and explore: You are never too old for learning and discovery. Open your mind. Study something you always wanted to know about but that didn't seem necessary or practical - other cultures and times, comparative religion, whatever calls you.

5. Volunteer: Nothing works better for relieving self-pity than helping others who are worse off. Fill the time you would have spent feeling sorry for yourself by giving something of yourself to others.

6. Get away: If you can possibly afford it, take a trip with a group of compatible people - perhaps a spiritual journey. Also, ask what is tying you to the community where you currently reside. Now is a time to consider the question of where, and how, you really want to live.

Believe in yourself. You have free will. You, and only you, are responsible for your life.

78 - Honor Diversity - Manage Prejudice

Everyone is a prisoner of his own experiences. No one can eliminate prejudices - just recognize them.
- Edward R. Murrow

Try a new perspective on diversity. Across the country and around the world, we are all one.

We are all "neighbors." Our world has gotten too small for us to be anything else. We can no longer have "us" and "them" - friends and enemies. A person from Iraq, or Russia, or Columbia is no more a stranger or enemy than a person from across town. A few people everywhere are troublemakers. Every religion provokes a few people to become extremists. Do we need police around the globe? Unfortunately, we always will. Do we need war? Does that question even deserve an answer?

I never considered a difference of opinion in politics, in religion, in philosophy, as cause for withdrawing from a friend.
- Thomas Jefferson

Open your mind to new thoughts. Pack your ancient and honored traditions respectfully, and store them in the attic of your past, to remember on days of reminiscence.

Open your heart to diversity. Love everyone without prejudice or bias. Honor the trainings of your youth by choosing to reinforce the lessons of universal love, while discarding the lessons of fear and exclusion.

Love and honor yourself, those with whom you feel close, those who challenge you, and those you have yet to meet. Make it a conscious daily practice to love and honor yourself and all others.

Happiness blooms where minds and hearts are open,
in the presence of self-respect and the absence of ego.

Life is all in the perspective we take on it.

Exercise: Let today be a day to look at your life from different and broader perspectives. This would be a good day to look at your live from a perspective of thankfulness for what you have and a perspective of wonder at your very existence and the magnificence of the world in which you live.

79 - Experiment With Your Perspective

Do you always look at life from the same point-of-view? Consider viewing a situation as another might view it. Look from behind, underneath, from the distant heavens. View the situation as someone of a different religion, race, or nationality might view it. Pretend you are an alien from a distant galaxy - that should be good for a laugh. Troubles only appear troubling to those close to them.

Where there is shouting, there is no true knowledge.
 - Leonardo da Vinci

Thoughtful people seldom share exactly the same opinion - the same point-of-view. The wise ones understand that they know nothing - for virtually none of our experience is truly factual - and they graciously honor all other opinions.

Arguing is merely defending one's opinion by labeling it, "Fact" or "The Truth."

There are no facts, only interpretations.
 - Friedrich Nietzsche

What we see depends more on ourselves than on what is "out there." We see what we assume (believe) will be there. We see what we expect (demand) to be there. We see what we fear will be there. And we see what we wish will be there. Then we label what we "see" as facts.

Wherever there are disagreements and confrontations, there are at least two perfectly valid interpretations that are vehemently labeled as "fact." Everyone considers "I'm right, you're wrong," to be a fact - the only difference is to whom "I" and "you" refer.

We don't see things as they are,
 we see things as we are. - Anaïs Nin

80 - See With New Eyes

Everything has beauty, but not everyone sees it.
- Confucius

A flower is a weed seen through joyful eyes.

The beauty does not live out there; the beauty's in my eyes.

The quality of life is in how we view it. We see a miserable, evil, and threatening world when we look through unhappy eyes. We see a vibrant, exciting, and hopeful world through joyful eyes.

We see Life through the fun-house mirrors of our point-of-view.

We never see Life as it really is. All we can ever see is the reflection of Life - distorted by our unique perceptions.

See beauty in the familiar

Look closely... See with new eyes... Don't just pass by what is familiar without a thought. Pay attention and look closely. There is beauty - there is discovery - there in a whole new world hiding behind the face of the familiar.

See that large animal chewing its cud and saying moo... the black and white one, or maybe the brown one. What do you see? Perhaps an object of religious veneration? Perhaps a friend to be decked in flowers and led through the streets on parade? Perhaps a source of milk? Perhaps tonight's pot roast? These are all the same animal, the difference is in our seeing.

What we see is more a function of our parents, our childhood, our family, our friends, our church, and our community than it is a direct result of the object or action before our eyes.

Moreover, we see what we ASSUME we will see. If you believe the world is evil, you will see evil. If you believe the world is good, you will see good. To change how life looks, change how you see life - change your expectations of life.

The virtue of anyone or anything is solely in our perspective. See gold, and there is gold; see lead and there is lead. If you see a thistle as a thorny nuisance, then it is a weed. If you appreciate its bright pink bloom, then it is a flower. It becomes what you name it. The power is in your choice, your perspective, your speaking.

81 - Ask Questions and Question Your Questions.

We Gain All Genuine Insight From Questions and Experiments.

Ask questions. If you don't like the answers, ask different questions.

True insight usually comes from asking great questions rather than finding great answers. Question every assumption & expectation

When a question appears to have no acceptable answer, it is a good time to consider asking a different question. Every question is based on some assumptions - usually invisible assumptions that we don't see, unless we go looking.

"How can I get my boss to give me the raise I deserve and need?" is that sort of question. Question the question. What are my priorities in life? How do I value money relative to play, family, friends, health? How could I redesign my life to need less money? Whatever your questions are, question them.

82 - Make Conscious Choosing a Way of Life

Faith is powerful, but it is no substitute for observing, paying attention, weighing alternatives, and choosing with intention. Without conscious choice, there is no freedom or happiness.

Honor tradition AND question tradition.
- Jonathan Lockwood Huie

"We've always done it that way." Whether a belief about how things should be done dates back two years, or twenty, or two thousand years, tradition neither confirms nor invalidates the usefulness of that belief.

Tradition is like a second-hand store. It is best to sort carefully between the treasures and the trash.

Decide questions without regard for tradition - one way or the other.

Today is your day to practice keen awareness. See everything with new eyes.

Today is a unique and special day. It is unlike any other day you have ever experienced. If you assume that today is like yesterday, you will never notice today's uniqueness. If you practice keen awareness, you will get to savor today's uniquely wonderful qualities.

We are responsible for the consequences of our choices - whether we choose with consciousness or we choose from habit. Conscious awareness and choice lead to joy.

83 - Beware the Rattlesnake of the Mind

Beware the Rattlesnake of the Mind

You are not your mind. You, a Spiritual BEing, are neither your mind nor your body. Mind and body are your tools - to use as you choose. Sometimes your body appears to have a will of its own, as when it twitches or pains. Likewise, your mind often appears to have its own will. That incessant chattering of regret, disappointment, guilt, shame, foreboding, worry, and fear is your Rattlesnake Mind striking off on its own.

Know that your mind can be a vicious rattlesnake, and be cautious. The mind can be tamed, but only with conscious effort and patience.

Beware the rattlesnake of the mind
- Jonathan Lockwood Huie

84 - Don't Believe Yourself.

Believe nothing, no matter where you read it, or who said it, no matter if I have said it, unless it agrees with your own reason and your own common sense.
 - The Buddha

Don't believe me. Don't believe yourself. Don't believe anybody else.
 - don Miguel Ruiz

Liar is a strong word, but we are all liars. Not in the sense of intentionally speaking untruths, but in the sense of carrying so much historical and emotional baggage that none of us is believable. To lie means to speak an untruth, and virtually everything that comes out of our mouth is an untruth - an opinion, an assumption, a point-of-view based on our past.

Try-on don Miguel's idea and never believe that anyone's speaking - especially your own - is the literal truth. Consider all ideas as interesting points-of-view that are worth considering and may prove useful - nothing more.

Believe nothing, no matter where you read it, or who said it, no matter if I have said it, unless it agrees with your own reason and your own common sense.
- the Buddha

85 - Open Your Mind to New Ways of Thinking

A question is asked and the answer returns, "Because we've always done it that way." Perhaps that isn't the most inspiring answer possible, but it actually reflects at least a moment's consideration of the question, and that's a good thing. Why do you drive a Ford? Because my family has always owned Fords. OK by me.

But when a question is asked and the answer is, "Huh?" we are dealing with something of an entirely different nature. Let's say you are an American male, and the question is, "Why do you wear pants and a shirt?" "Huh?" Perhaps the actual answer is a snotty, "Because I'd look funny in a dress," but it still means, "Huh? That's not even a question." Of course the reason virtually all American males go into the world in pants and shirt rather than dresses, kilts, kimonos, jumpsuits, pajamas, bathrobe, or whatever is that virtually all the other American males wear pants and shirt. Purely cultural.

You're Christian (most denominations), "Why do you take off your hat in church?" "Respect." "How is taking off your hat respectful?" "Huh?" You're Jewish, "Why do you wear a yarmulke (hat) in Synagogue?" "Respect." "How is wearing a hat respectful?" "Huh?" Of course religious experts would be ready to reference some ancient text as "answer" to the question, but that's just another way of saying, "Because my culture has always done it that way."

The point is NOT that we SHOULD do anything differently from the way we have "always done it." In many cases it would be downright foolhardy to buck cultural norms. That the people of some political unit agree to drive on the right (or left) side of the highway is purely cultural, like agreeing to wear or not wear head covering during worship. However, a unilateral personal decision to choose to drive on the other side of the road would risk a fine, imprisonment, or grave bodily harm. The same is true for choosing not to pay taxes, or refusing military conscription or jury duty.

This secret is not about changing what we do, it's about thinking, about awareness, and about choosing. Become AWARE of the cultural norms that pervade our lives. THINK about the alternatives. CHOOSE, based on free-will.

Usually, our free-will choice will be to do exactly the same as our parents and our family and our neighbors. Great! Choosing to drive on the same side of the roadway as our neighbors is going to prevent a great deal of conflict.

However, surprisingly often, starting to question our cultural norms will open new vistas for us. Perhaps something as simple as a Northerner discovering they love okra and gumbo. Maybe something as life-altering as the revelation of preferring not to become a parent, or choosing to live on a boat or in an RV rather than a fixed location.

86 - Have a "Beginner Mind"

A newborn does not have worry, or stress, or anger, because they have not yet learned those things. Consider what life would be like if you could forget all the past resentments and perceived offenses that color your thinking and your emotions. Buddhists call that state "beginner mind" - an opening to experience life without the jaundiced filter of past disappointments.

Shed the scales from your eyes

Bringing a childlike wonder and a beginner's mind to life maximize both success and joy.

Over the years, we experience disappointments, and then develop a fear of the unfamiliar. We make assumptions about how things ARE. We make expectations of others and of ourselves based on those assumptions.

"Beginner Mind" is a Zen Buddhist term that describes moving past our assumptions of the nature of our life, and really SEEING our surroundings - especially the people we interact with - with new eyes.

Maybe life isn't really as complicated as we make it out to be. Perhaps a simple child-like attitude would create a less stressful and happier life.

Choose to be as a young child - fully awake, eager for the next experience.

Consciously adopt the mindset of a young child, to whom all of life is a grand adventure. Life is your playground, fashion grand castles and sweeping boulevards, defeat fire-breathing dragons and leap tall buildings in a single bound.

87 - Become Your Own Personal Greatest Hero

To go against the dominant thinking of your friends, of most of the people you see every day, is perhaps the most difficult act of heroism you can perform.
- Theodore H. White

Who do we most respect and admire? Why our Heroes of course. What are the characteristics of a Hero? Heroes are courageous and self-reliant, and they are greatly admired. Being courageous and self-reliant are the characteristics that create heroes. Being admired is something that comes afterward.

Name a genuine Hero who followed the crowd? It's a crazy question, because Heroes don't follow the crowd. A hero may or may not lead other people, but all heroes lead themselves.

Heroes are self confident independent thinkers who make courageous choices. By committing their entire focus to their goals, Heroes leave no time or energy for worry or self-inflicted emotional suffering. Heroism is a path to a joyful life as well as to inspired service.

Want to be a Hero, just pick one to emulate - WRONG. To be heroic, don't emulate a hero, learn from one. Heroes don't follow anyone, they set their own course.

A leader is most effective when people barely know he exists. When his work is done, his aim fulfilled, his troops will feel they did it themselves.
- Lao Tzu

Exercise: Who is your Personal Greatest Hero? Take pen and paper. Write why you admire your greatest hero, and which of their qualities inspire you.

88 - Begin the Practice of a Silent Daily Walk

Everybody needs beauty as well as bread, places to play in and pray in where nature may heal and cheer and give strength to the body and soul.
- John Muir

Begin each day with a silent walk: Get up a half hour earlier to make time for it. While a walk in a natural setting is ideal, a walk on city streets will do fine.

Thoughts, angers, resentments, and fears will form in your mind as you walk. That "mind chatter" is always with us whenever we are not focused on a specific mental activity, and it gets much stronger when we are stressed. Neither resent the mind chatter, nor let it linger. Say "thank you" to each passing thought, anger, resentment, or fear - then release it and return to your silent walk.

There is sanctuary in being alone with nature.

There is sanctuary in being alone with nature.
- Jonathan Lockwood Huie

89 - Dance Lightly With Life

Today is your day to dance lightly with life. It really is.
Today is your day to dance lightly with life,
sing wild songs of adventure,
invite rainbows & butterflies out to play,
soar your spirit, and unfurl your joy.

Smile. Today would be a wonderful day not to take life so seriously. Today may end up the way you prefer - and it may not. Happiness is not about being a winner - it's about being gentle with life - being gentle with yourself. Let life be a dance, and choose the kind of dance you want for today - perhaps a gentle loving dance.

Life does not have to be a serious undertaking. You will make mistakes, you will feel regrets, and eventually, you will die - so what? Happiness comes from dancing lightly with life - playing hopscotch on the river of life - leaping gracefully from joy to joy while laughing at the threats of calamity - even laughing hysterically at our human frailness when we do fall into the muddy torrent.

Imagine, Play, Turn Cartwheels, Be Unstoppable, Dance Wildly With Life.

The moment you start seeing life as non-serious, a playfulness, all the burden on your heart disappears. All the fear of death, of life, of love - everything disappears.
- Osho

Life is a game - a game you can never win. You already know the final score: Life 1, You 0.

The great news is that the game can be wonderful fun while it lasts, as long as you remember that it is a game and keep it light and playful. Tease life, taunt life, never attack life head-on.

I Dance through Life with a Light Heart.

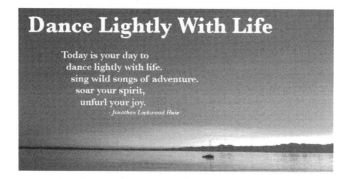

90 - Know That Life is NOT SUPPOSED to be Fair

There is a secret wisdom-of-the-ages that holds the key to breaking our cycle of self-imposed suffering. That secret wisdom is, "Life was never intended to be fair."

This is not sad news. This is GLORIOUS news! Life is not broken. Nothing is wrong. God has not failed, died, or gone on vacation. The world is working perfectly. We just misunderstood.

Somewhere along the way, someone got the idea that life was "supposed" to be "fair," and all the trouble started - expectation, disappointment, resentment, anger - a whole cycle of suffering that began with the belief that life is "supposed" to be "fair."

If you still think that life is supposed to be fair, read National Geographic or watch Animal Planet. Humans are not exempt from the nature of life.

We admit to our children at a fairly young age that the Tooth Fairy and Santa Clause are fairy tales. Why not prevent immeasurable suffering and confess to our children at that same age that life is not supposed to be fair?

Know that there is no single way that life is "supposed" to be. Demanding that life meet our expectations is a sure fire recipe for a miserable existence.

Life is a game with no rules. The joy of life comes from playing the game of life as best we can, focusing far more on the love and good example we can contribute to other lives than on demanding money, possessions, love, or appreciation.

Life is a constant opponent, and an overpowering adversary if attacked directly. The successful and happy ones dance lightly with life - a parry here, a feint there - always engaged, but never in the direct line of life's heaviest blows.

Life just happens to us regardless of our best intentions. Our only path to happiness lies in being open to receiving whatever life throws at us - with Gratitude.

Have NO Expectations of life.

91 - Don't Attempt to Make Life "Fair"

You don't have the power to make life "fair," but you do have the power to make life joyful.

"I did the dishes, you need to take out the garbage." "You borrowed money from me, you need to pay it back." "My broker told me the market would go up, and just look." "It's not fair."

"Fair" is not a useful concept. Life is not "fair." You can't make life "fair." You can get angry. You can complain about life not being "fair." You can attempt revenge - perhaps violently. You can inflict great suffering upon yourself in the name of life being "unfair."

Get over it. Life isn't "fair." You can choose anger, resentment, revenge and suffering, or you can choose joy.

Life is not supposed to be fair.

Identify your assumptions (what you believe) about "fairness." Question how you feel when you hold those assumptions. Visualize holding different assumptions. Ask yourself how it feels to hold a different world-view about how things "should be."

Life is as easy or as hard as you think it is

Whenever you say or even think, "This is hard," that task or challenge becomes difficult. Dread it, and it becomes terrifying.

Life is as easy or
as hard as you
think it is
- Jonathan Lockwood Huie

92 - Be Playful

We don't stop playing because we grow old; we grow old because we stop playing.
- George Bernard Shaw

Do not take life too seriously. You will never get out of it alive.
- Elbert Hubbard

Life is to be taken lightly - by those who wish to be happy and by those who wish to age gracefully.

Do you remember Cloud Animals? Be a child again

I remember warm summer afternoons, laying in the shade of a maple tree in the back yard of my Connecticut home watching the clouds for hours. As those clouds formed dragons and foxes, clowns and angels, I traveled across space and time.

When was the last time you let your imagination run completely unchecked? Unfetter your inner child and let her or him run wild today.

We don't stop playing because we grow old; we grow old because we stop playing.
- George Bernard Shaw

93 - Celebrate Whimsy Today

Today is your day to dance lightly with life,
invite rainbows & butterflies out to play.
Today is your day to practice whimsy,
watch wondrous cloud animals parade your story,
find a magical white bunny down every rabbit hole.

Who made the rule that life has to be so serious? One would think that "life is serious" had been engraved upon stone tablets to judge from how most lives are lived. Get a life, smile broadly, sing loudly, paint your rooms in bold colors, search every rabbit hole for a magical white bunny, have caviar for breakfast and oatmeal for dinner, wear a purple coat with a red hat - dance lightly with life.

Most of us seldom let the outrageous part of ourselves out to play, but what if we like our outrageous side best? We "know" that the "right" thing to do is to suck it up, put the costume and the happy face back in storage for another year, re-dress in our frown and gray flannel suit, and trudge back to job, chores, "responsibilities," and "duty."

Maybe TODAY is the day to put the frown and gray flannel into that dusty storage locker, and start to LIVE. Not just today, but EVERY DAY for the rest of your life!

Celebrate today... Celebrate ME... Celebrate Life... Celebrate Rainbows & Butterflies... Celebrate Whimsy...

When was the last time you blew bubbles? Flew a kite? Skipped down the road? Laughed for no reason until you rolled on the floor? Unless you have small children and take the time to play with them, it may have been a while.

Take off your shoes and dance on the beach... Play in the mud... Sing at the top of your lungs... and don't care who hears you.

Grin your smile; giggle your laugh; unfurl your joy; dash the last trace of your self-consciousness; and cavort your most uninhibited play.

Exercise: Today, do something Outrageous - just because you want to.

94 - Appreciate Quiet Moments

Silence is a source of great strength.
- Lao Tzu

It's foggy and it's gray - let's play.

For both the weather outside, and the weather of our inner life, foggy and gray can be fully as much cause for joy and play as sunshine and blue skies. There is as much joy in a cup of hot chocolate and a roaring fire as in a day at the beach; as much joy in a quiet day with a book as in closing that long awaited business deal.

Life comes in quiet moments and grand ones. Our joy always occurs in our perceptions of our lives, rather than in the events themselves.

May the world be kind to you, and
may your own thoughts
be gentle upon yourself.
- Jonathan Lockwood Huie

95 - Laugh at Yourself

Today is your day to laugh at life,
laugh loud - laugh often,
laugh at what's funny - laugh at what's sad,
laugh at me - laugh at you - laugh at life.

Lighten up! Your greatest gift to your family and friends is yourself - your relaxed, happy, and fully-present self.

Life's burdens are lighter when I laugh at myself.

Life's burdens are lighter when I laugh at myself.

- Jonathan Lockwood Huie

96 - Become Creative and Artistic (yes you can)

Today is your day to paint life in bold colors,
set today's rhythm with your heart-drum,
walk today's march with courage,
create today as your celebration of life.

Out with the gray! In with color; in with the juice of life.

Vision - Creation - Art? Each of us is an artist, but many are repressed artists. There is something of ourselves that cannot be expressed in words. Perhaps that something can be expressed in form or color, dance or music. If only with crayons or a tin drum, let that something that cannot be said move your hands or your body today.

Today is your day to paint life in bold colors, set today's rhythm with your heart-drum, walk today's march with courage, create today as your celebration of life.
- Jonathan Lockwood Huie

painting by Suze Stewart

97 - Tame Anxiety By Using the Qigong Release Exercise

Spirit is always ready to lighten our burdens. Our only job is to ask respectfully. Here is a ceremony for releasing your troubles back to the Universe.

This exercise releases both your attachment to those things that haunt you, and your attachment to the fear of losing what you do not believe you can live without.

Choose a quiet place, and stand comfortably with feet spread slightly apart. Take a deep breath, and exhale with a resonant mmmm... sound. Bend slightly at the waist and reach down with both hands - with hands facing each other and about 6 inches apart.

Choose something that is very important to you and that you don't think you could stand to lose - such as your house, your favorite sport, your pet, your relationship with a loved one, your hearing, your eyesight, your life. Visualize your important something between your hands.

Rise slowly and bring your hands to your heart - still 6 inches apart, and still holding your treasure. Feel intense love and gratitude for every joyful instant that you have spent with your important something. Now slowly raise your hands above your head, spread your hands apart, and RELEASE your treasure back to the Universe. It never belonged to you anyway - it was just on short term loan from Spirit.

Choose another important something and release it. For everything important in your life, pick it up, love it, nurture it, give thanks for it, and then release it.

Do the same exercise for each person that you have ever loved, and that has passed from this life. Hold them, love them, give thanks for them, and then release them back to the Universe.

Now, release your burdens - your fears, regrets, guilts, shames, embarrassments, angers. One by one, pick up each memory or fear that troubles you, hold it close, and release it to the Universe. Release each incident from your past that still bothers you. Release each fear - your fears about your health, your family, your job, and every other fear.

Breathe deeply, and give thanks.

98 - Release Your Concerns to the Cleansing Fire

Release Your Anger, Resentment, and Fear to the Cleansing Fire
The cleansing fire of Spirit consumes the troubles of this world.
Feed your concerns to the fire. Breathe deeply and rejoice.

Release your angers, resentments, and fears by feeding your troubles and fears to the cleansing fire: Light a candle or small fire. Write one trouble or fear on a piece of paper, and feed it to the fire, while releasing the issue to Spirit. Repeat until you can no longer think of another issue that burdens you.

Trust in the Light.

Darkness is not a force - it is merely the absence of light. Observe that when a light is brought to a dark place, the darkness disappears. Sadness is similar - when joy is brought to suffering, the sadness disappears.

Open yourself to the Light! Hold back nothing, Trust in the Light.

Exercise: Write your most worrisome trouble on a piece of paper and feed it to the fire. Send your troubles up in smoke. Breathe deeply and rejoice.

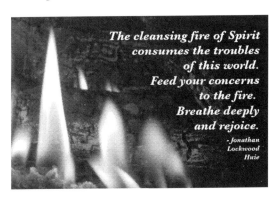

The cleansing fire of Spirit consumes the troubles of this world. Feed your concerns to the fire. Breathe deeply and rejoice.

- Jonathan Lockwood Huie

99 - Connect with Your Higher Power

Today is your day to see in yourself the face of god.
Your mind sparks, your soul sparkles.
Your peace is counterpoint to the clamor of life.
You are a magnificent gift to the world.

There are only two ways to live your life. One is as though nothing is a miracle. The other is as though everything is a miracle.
  - Albert Einstein

What is a miracle? To some, it is an act of God. To others, something amazing, extraordinary, or unexpected. To me, Life is a miracle. Everything that happens is a miracle. There is no reason for me to exist as I do - no reason for humanity, the universe, or the laws of Nature. Energy, mass, gravity and the rest of existence are all so improbable.

Every day I give thanks that I am me, and that everything that has ever occurred in my life happened exactly as it did - however unpleasant it may have appeared at the time.

There are only two ways to live your life. One is as though nothing is a miracle. The other is as though everything is a miracle. *- Albert Einstein*

100 - Feel Unity with Spirit and All Creation

All things share the same breath - the beast, the tree, the man... the air shares its spirit with all the life it supports.
- Chief Seattle

When I see Spirit in Everything, Peace is at hand.

When I see Spirit in everything, Peace is at hand.
-Jonathan Lockwood Huie

UNITY - we are all one - the web of life.

You are never alone. Your Higher Power, whatever that means to you, is a constant support - never hesitate to ask for guidance and blessing.

Remember that Spirit knows better than you what is best for you, so ask for comfort and affluence rather than the affections of a particular person or a higher paying job. Whatever your circumstances, and however often you may have felt rejected, there are many people in this world who live in the tradition of the "Good Samaritan." When troubles weigh upon you, do not hesitate to find and rely upon these people - they are far more numerous than you think.

Know Unity With Spirit: There are as many ways to connect with Spirit as there are people - each of us has our own way to receive strength and serenity from the Infinite. Your life will be happier if you acknowledge that you are not alone, become open to that presence, and create ritual to celebrate your connection.

You may feel your bond with Spirit at the Lord's Supper, in Songs of Praise, in Calls to Prayer, in Meditation, while doing Yoga or Qigong, or while walking in the woods. However you connect with Spirit, do it today.

When the vast cathedral of our being becomes a sanctuary for all creation, we become the face of God.

My wish, today, for each of you is Joy, Honor, acceptance of diversity, and Unity with Spirit and All Creation.

May your spirit soar throughout the vast cathedral of your being.
May your mind whirl joyful cartwheels of creativity.
May your heart sing sweet lullabies of timelessness.

more Positive Affirmations

by Jonathan Lockwood Huie

- I Live a Life of Bold and Courageous Action Inspired by Powerful Dreams.

- I Dream with Powerful Intention.

- I open my mind to Spirit,

- I trust my intuition to deliver powerful visions of my inspired future, and I empower my intent to transform those visions into reality.

- I honor all people and cultures.

- I choose to live a life of gratitude and joy, inspiring others to follow my example.

- I play with life, laugh with life, dance lightly with life, and smile at the riddles of life, knowing that life's only true lessons are writ small in the margin.

- There is nothing I ever need to have.

- There is nothing I ever need to do.

- I Say NO to the demands of the world.

- I Say YES to the longings of my own heart.

- I make friends with my fear. I am unstoppable.

- Today is my day to dance lightly with life.

- I soar high above the troubles of the world.

- I sing wild songs of adventure.

- I invite rainbows & butterflies out to play.

- I soar my spirit, and unfurl my joy.

- Today is my day to honor my being,

- I release each and every struggle.

- I gather strength from life's storms.

- I relax into the arms of spirit.

- Today Is My Day To Laugh At Life.

- Today is my day to laugh loud - laugh often

- Today is my day to paint life in bold colors.

- Today, I will be gentle with myself.

- I set today's life-rhythm with my heart-drum.

- I walk today's march with courage,

- I create today as my celebration of life.

- Today is my day to practice whimsey,

- I skip on the beach, and play with the wave.

- I watch wondrous cloud animals parade my story.

- I find a magical white bunny down every rabbit hole.

- Today is my day to see in myself the face of god.

- My mind sparks, my soul sparkles.

- My peace is counterpoint to the clamor of life.

- Today, I Dance Lightly With Life.

- I ascend from Fear to Unconditional Love.

Jonathan Lockwood Huie and Mary Anne Radmacher's inspiring self-help book is available now from Conari Press.

Simply An Inspired Life:

Consciously Choosing Unbounded Happiness in Good Times and Bad
by Jonathan Lockwood Huie and Mary Anne Radmacher

Are you unhappy, or worried about the future? Does it seem that the whole world is conspiring against you? Your boss? Your spouse? Your family? The government? The economy?

It is possible to enjoy a happy life, even in the face of life's most challenging circumstances. Let *Simply An Inspired Life* be your guide to a joyful life - your beacon of hope in a troubled and confusing world.

Take time out to pamper your mind and spirit. This is the perfect self-awareness book to help you to see and be grateful for what is good in life. Tips, techniques, feel-good stories, and uplifting quotes will make your days more joyful.

"*Simply An Inspired Life* comes to the rescue. It offers not just permission to slow down and get a life, but clear instructions on how to do just that."
- Victoria Moran, author of *Living a Charmed Life: Your Guide to Finding Magic in Every Moment of Every Day*

"Jonathan and Mary Anne remind us that life is so much more than work, school, making money, paying bills -- there are rainbows after the rain, there is sunlight that lights our path, there is laughter and smiles, there are the first steps of a child, there are so many beautiful things to focus on." - a reader

Life change comes about in two complementary ways - the "aha" moment, which occurs in a flash of insight, and the conscious redesigning of our habitual behaviors, which is a lifelong project. *Simply An Inspired Life* addresses both the flash of insight that suffering is optional, and the structural pillars that support living an inspired life.

Chapter two describes a powerful technique for personal transformation called "Breaking the Cycle of Self-Inflicted Suffering". The reader is gently guided through identifying the relationship of perceived scarcity to suffering, and then coached in breaking that painful cycle.

The remainder of the book introduces and develops the Eight Points that are the pillars of Simply An Inspired Life.

Eight Points of An Inspired Life - Keys to Happiness

* HONOR for true self.
* FORGIVENESS for self and all.
* GRATITUDE in everything.
* CHOICE with open mind and heart.
* VISION with powerful intention.
* ACTION with bold courage.
* CELEBRATION with joy.
* UNITY with all creation.

Read more about *Simply An Inspired Life* and order at
www.SimplyAnInspiredLife.com or from your favorite bookseller.

Jonathan Lockwood Huie's On-line Happiness Training Program is now available at www.DreamThisDay.com/happiness-program/

Regaining Your Happiness in Seven Weeks
e-Training Program
by Jonathan Lockwood Huie
49 Daily Lessons delivered by email, plus introductory video

Does everyday life frustrate and annoy you?

Do people, circumstances, and life in general seem to conspire against you?

Suppose there were a way to regain your happiness?

Well there IS a way to regain your happiness! And you don't have to win the lottery or even get a salary increase to get your happiness back.

The *Regaining Your Happiness in Seven Weeks* e-Training Program is designed to reduce your emotional suffering and increase the joy you find in everyday living by helping you to:

1. Understand the role your past plays in triggering your current emotional state.
2. Access the power of forgiveness and gratitude to create happiness.
3. Establish a framework for designing your inspired future.

Your 49 Lessons of this program will be delivered by email each day for the next seven weeks. Every day, you will receive a concise insight into that day's issue. Each lesson features one or more daily exercises that give life to that insight during the course of your normal day's activities.

Does the *Regaining Your Happiness in Seven Weeks* e-Training Program really work? Here is praise for the Regaining Your Happiness Program from those who have experienced it...

I can't even start to put into words how much this series helped me. It seemed nothing could get worse, and battling suicidal thoughts had become a constant issue. When I found the *Regaining Your Happiness in Seven Weeks* Series, I half-heartedly signed up. Figuring there was nothing to lose at that point, I began to read a little bit each day. Some days, it was too much effort, but I did what I could. Now, a few months later, the depression is lifting, I have a sense of worth again, and I believe I will be ok! *Regaining Your Happiness in Seven Weeks* has certainly been a big part of my recovery. I go back and re-read the lessons from time to time,

and quite often, I get something a little different than before. This is a program I've suggested to many others, and I am eternally grateful for having found it!
Thank you, Jonathan, for caring enough to share!
Vickie, Murfreesboro, TN

I looked forward to your e-training each day that my friend and I were going through life transitions and particularly challenging life experiences. It is amazing how you begin to depend on them and let their benefit greet and improve your day.!
Fran

Your program dovetailed quite nicely with my 12 Step Program (Nar-Anon). In fact, I chaired a meeting using some of your ideas on forgiveness. Very powerful. I enjoyed working on the daily assignments especially revisiting childhood. I thank you for offering your Happiness Training Program. I recommend it to my friends.
Cindy T, Pittsburgh, PA

Thank you for letting me participate in the Happiness in Seven Weeks e-training. It truly was inspirational! I found the content very useful. It helped me through a difficult time in my life. Thank you again for the INSPIRATION & ENCOURAGEMENT.
Sally, Cincinnati

Read more about the *Regaining Your Happiness in Seven Weeks* e-Training Program and order at www.DreamThisDay.com/happiness-program/

5481009R0

Made in the USA
Lexington, KY
13 May 2010